Making

God

Real

in the Orthodox

Christian Home

May your Home be a mini-church!

Love
Kusann +
Evttlyn

LIGHT & LIFE PUBLISHING COMPANY
MINNEAPOLIS, MINNESOTA

Light & Life Publishing Company
P.O. Box 26421
Minneapolis, MN 55426-0421

Revised and expanded 2004.

ISBN 0-937032-07-7

Table of Contents

What the Bible Says About Children

Fathers, do not exasperate your children; instead bring them up in the training and instruction of the Lord.

-Ephesians 6:4

Whoever welcomes a little child . . . in my name welcomes me. But if anyone causes one of these little ones who believe in me to sin, it would be better for him to have a large millstone hung around his neck and to be drowned in the depths of the sea.

-Matthew 18:5-6

Let the children come to me, do not hinder them, for to such belongs the Kingdom of God.

-Mark 10:14

Truly, I say to you, whoever does not receive the Kingdom of God like a child shall not enter it. And he took them in his arms and blessed them, laying his hands upon them.

-Mark 10:15

Church Fathers on Child Rearing

Of all holy works, the education of children is the most holy.

-St. Theophan

Rear your children in the Lord . . . Teach them from infancy the Word of God. Discipline them when needed, and render them respectful to legitimate authority. Never let them exercise authority over you.

-The Apostolic Constitutions
(an early document of the Church)

If you mold her completely in this way, you will save not only her but also the husband who will marry her, not only the husband but also the children, not only the children but also the grandchildren. For when the root becomes good, the shoots are out-stretched toward what is better, and for all these you will receive the reward. Therefore, let us do all things so as to help not one soul alone, but many through the one.

-St. John Chrysostom

The primary lesson for life must be implanted in the soul from the earliest age. The primary lesson for children is to know the eternal God, the One Who gives everlasting life.

-St. Clement

Preface

Dr. Boojamra, noted Orthodox educator, wrote:

All we can do is educate our children into the church. We cannot educate them into faith, because that comes as an act of the will and an act of God's grace. There is no way an educational process can give the gift of faith. All we can do is prepare people to receive it, and that happens in the Church and in the home.

But one thing we must do. And that is to pray each day that our children will be moved by the Holy Spirit to open their hearts to receive the gift of faith. The child is a bridge connecting the mother to the father, so that three become one flesh, as when two cities divided by a river are joined by a bridge. If the child is a bridge connecting mother and father-just imagine how much traffic-conversation, prayer, interaction-should be passing over that bridge, serving to mold and make that child in the image of God. Thus, in reading and implementing the family practices outlined in this book, we need to follow the advice of the saint who said, "Pray as if everything depends on God, and work as if everything depends on you."

Foreword

I like to compare our relationships with our children to Lazarus after Jesus resurrected him and said to his friends, "Unbind him!" The friends began removing the grave clothes from Lazarus strip by strip, unwrapping him so he could move and take his place in the world. I like to look upon our children as coming to us from God all wrapped up. They need to be unbound by loving, caring parents. There are strips of insecurity, self-consciousness, lack of identity; strips of fear, and hurt that need to be peeled away to allow freedom of movement and action as our children proceed to go from baptism to the goal of theosis, i.e., becoming like God in Christ, sharing in His glory. Our Lord has given us many tasks, but I can think of none more important than that of helping unwrap those precious bundles He sends to us from heaven. "Of all holy works, the education of children is the most holy," said St. Theophan the Recluse.

-The Author

Family: The Great Ascetic Feat of Christianity

A young man who had entered a monastery wrote to his father and told him how wonderful it was to be there. Every morning at 3 o'clock the monks rise to chant ancient hymns. His father, a wise and thoughtful man, wrote back, "Dear Son: Your mother and I are so happy to know that you have found your vocation. But always remember one thing: We, too, and many parents like us living in the world, have arisen on numerous occasions at 3 o'clock in the morning to feed our babies or change diapers, and in the process have found our own vocation equally sacred." Indeed, most sacred!

Never let anyone tell you that the vocation of the monk or nun-important as they are-are more sacred than that of mom and dad at home, loving and training the children God gave them. Unlike the Roman Catholic Church, the Orthodox Church has not established formally a hierarchy of Christian life in which celibacy (the unmarried state of monks, nuns and priests) is designated a higher state of Christian living than marriage. In fact, married life and the raising of a family has been described at times within the Orthodox tradition as a more difficult and courageous vocation than that of celibacy. The domestic church-the family-is often called "the great ascetic feat of Christianity" (Dmitri Dudko). Clement of Alexandria wrote, "True manhood is shown not in the choice of a celibate life; on the contrary, the prize in the contest of men is won by him who has trained himself by the discharge of the duties of husband and father ..."

The Bible has a remarkable phrase, indicating that "through childbirth, a woman shall be saved." Whatever else this verse may mean, it points to a most important role in the life of the Church for women. The work of procreation is only begun with the child's birth. Procreation does not end with childbirth. Parents are continually creating life; continually creating personality in their children with the kind of family faith atmosphere they provide. Is there any task more sacred or more exalted than this? Parents have the awesome privilege of being able to "save" the world through this kind of childbirth, rearing, and nurturing.

The first icon of God the child sees is the face of mother and father. One person said, "Initially my parents and family were the church. They were the ones who conveyed faith to me, who nourished me not only physically but spiritually as well." Could this be why Chyrsostom called marriage "the mysterious icon of the Church"? And St. Paul called the home "the church in your house"? And could this be why Clement of Alexandria suggested that the two or three gathered in Christ's name among whom Christ is present (see Matt. 18:20) are "husband, wife and child"? Augustine had no doubt about this when he wrote of his mother Monica, "who brought me to birth both in her body so that I was born into the light of time, and in her heart so that I was born in the light of eternity."

A Parent's Prayer

"O Heavenly Father, make me a better parent. Teach me to understand my children, to listen patiently to what they have to say, and to answer all their questions kindly. Keep me from interrupting them or contradicting them. Make me as courteous to them as I would have them be to me. Forbid that I should ever laugh at their mistakes or resort to shame or ridicule when they displease me. May I never punish them for my own selfish satisfaction or to show my power. Let me not tempt my children to lie or steal. And guide me hour by hour that I may demonstrate by all that I say and do that honesty produces happiness. Reduce, I pray, the meanness in me. And when I'm out of sorts, help me, O Lord, to hold my tongue. May I ever be mindful that my children are children and I should not expect of them the judgment of adults. Let me not rob them of the opportunity to wait on themselves and to make decisions. Bless me with the bigness to grant them all their reasonable requests and the courage to deny them privileges I know will do them harm. Make me fair and just and kind and fit, O Lord, to be loved and respected and imitated by my children. Amen."

Who Is Raising the Children?

Violence and vandalism in the nation's public schools are approaching epidemic proportions-and nobody seems to know what to do about it.

More than 30% of school-age children are living with parents who have been divorced at least once. Due to rising rates of divorce, desertion and illegitimacy, one sixth of all U.S. children under 18 live in one-parent families.

Who is raising the children?

Six million pre-school children have working mothers.

The "extended family"-in which grandparents and other adults once handled many child-rearing duties-is fast disappearing. Now we have what is called the nuclear family of just parents and children which is often dominated by what one psychologist calls the "flickering blue parent-television," serving as babysitter, educator, mind-former and electronic tranquilizer.

Who is raising the children?

At least one million young Americans run away from home every year. Suicide is the second-leading cause of death for young Americans between the ages of 15 and 24. One out of nine youths ends up in juvenile court by age 18. Approximately 10 percent of all school-age children have moderate to severe mental and emotional problems. Drug abuse and alcoholism among teenagers are becoming serious public health problems.

Who is raising the children?

An authority on family life says,

"Television tends to help people run away from life. And TV constantly preaches materialism. Commercials say consumption of goods is the purpose of human existence. In many homes both parents have to work to supply the money to buy all these material goods. If both parents work eight hours a day, they don't have a lot left to give to themselves and to the kids."

"Latchkey" children, who return to empty houses after school to await their parents' return from work, run into the millions.

Who is raising the children?

Is secular society raising them? Are the movies raising them? Are porn magazines raising them?

Where do our children receive their values? How do they learn to evaluate and judge for themselves the things they meet and hear?

Many will ask, "Well, what's the church for? Isn't this the church's responsibility?" How much time do children spend in Sunday school and church? If they come regularly, 36 hours a year! That adds up to about a day and a half a year! In whose hands are they supposed to be the remainder of the time? The parents! And those parents who drop their children off for church school and church should not be surprised when the children follow in their footsteps and become what their parents are-drop-outs.

Who is raising the children?

We hear much today about the subject of women priests. Why don't we ordain women as priests? Why should we? God has already ordained them into the sacred priesthood of motherhood. Who can ever be a more effective priest to her children than a dedicated Christian mother? We talk about the inequality of the sexes. It is not a matter of difference in equality of nature. It is a matter of difference in function. No one can ever take a mother's place in the home. No one is endowed by God as she is for the raising of children. We need to emphasize this point. For, we are trying to do every-thing we can today to take mothers out of homes, to destroy the sacred priesthood of motherhood, and leave the home front unattended. This, in itself, is producing so many prob-lems that it could very well lead to the downfall of our nation.

A Harvard researcher discovered recently that "superkids"-outstanding achievers are reared in homes where parents talk a lot to their children and do not rely on televi-sion. They act as the children's "personal consultants," respond to their questions and discipline them firmly and effectively.

The church can do nothing without the home. The most influential school in the world is not Oxford or Harvard or the Sorbonne or Yale or Cambridge. It is the home.

The question is not, "Is there a school under your roof?" The real question is, "How good is the school under your roof?" What are you teaching? What are you not teaching?

If you think all of this talk about the home is putting a terrifying amount of responsibility on the home, you're right.

Listen to what the Bible says about the home:

"Hear, O Israel, the Lord our God is one Lord; and you shall love the Lord your God with all your heart and with all your soul, and with all your might. And these words which I command you this day shall be upon your heart; and you shall teach them diligently to your children, and shall talk of them when you sit in your house and when you walk by the way, and when you lie down, and when you rise" (Deut. 6:3-7).

"And you shall teach them diligently to your children"-not in Sunday school, not in church, but "*in your house*," says God's word.

If we do not learn to know and love God in the home, we

shall be sent out to face life totally unprepared, with no inner braces. And when we have no *inner* braces, we go around looking for *outer* braces such as alcohol or drugs.

The faithful Orthodox Christian parent does not ask, "Who is raising the children?" He knows this to be his/her most solemn and sacred God-given privilege and responsibility.

If the one hour a week spent in church and church school is to be effective, it must be supplemented in that greatest of all schools-the home-by informed, dedicated Christian parents who, by family discussions, family prayer, a special family evening, family Bible reading, and family devotions at the supper table will give their children the greatest gift possible: the knowledge of the One, True God in Christ Jesus Who will walk with them through life, strengthen them, heal them, guide them, give meaning to their life, grant them the peace of God and lead them ultimately to life eternal.

The purpose of this book is to help Orthodox Christian parents make God real in the home. Many ideas and methods are offered to equip parents to serve as priests to their children. The ideas offered are by no means exhaustive. You may have others that have worked well for you.

How the Orthodox Church Embraces the Child From Day One

May I share with you how royally the Orthodox Church welcomes a newborn child into her bosom from day one? It is as if the church, representing God and God's people, rushes out to welcome the newborn, saying, "We're so glad you're here!" On the day the birth takes place, the church prays for the mother who has just given birth and asks for protection for the child: "Grant, O Lord, that the child which hath been born of her may do reverence to the earthly temple which thou hast prepared to glorify thy holy Name." On the eighth day, the child receives its name, the name of a saint, "that the light of thy countenance may be shown upon thy servant." Through the giving of a name the child is recognized as a distinct and unique person. On the fortieth day, the mother brings the child to church, and the priest prays for it to receive spiritual light just as it now contemplates the natural light, "that in due season it may be united to thy holy flock." Then, at baptism, the child is immersed in the bath of regeneration. Plunged three times into the water the child shares in the death and resurrection of the Savior. It is identified with Christ. "For as many of you as have been baptized into Christ have put on Christ" (Galatians 3:27). Immediately afterward, anointing with the Spirit (the sacrament of Chrismation) makes the one baptized an authentic dwelling place of the Trinity. "Born again of water and the Spirit," a member of the Body of Christ, the child is now a full member of the Church. From that time on the child goes to Communion and receives "the bread of true life," the Body and Blood of the Lord.

Immediately following baptism, the church and the home

begin to work together to train this new member of Christ's Body to become "a champion for Jesus." What the child does at church, he can do at home: pray before the family icon, light the flame before the family icon, cense the home, be present at the annual blessing of the home by the priest, read at home the same Scripture lessons as are read in Church, assist in the daily blessing of meals, make the sign of the cross, receive the parent's blessing before leaving for school, participate in the fasting periods-these and many, many other Orthodox family traditions will keep the flame of faith burning in the heart of each child as he/she grows physically, mentally, and spiritually in favor with God and man.

A Weekly Family Home Evening

Harmon Killebrew, a famous Twins baseball player, belonged to a religious group which believes in attacking delinquency and declining morality by strengthening the family through a Monday night get-together in the home called the "family home evening."

This is the time, usually about 7 p.m., when his family prays together, sings together, talks about its problems together, plays games together, and then, usually, has an extra special dessert that was saved from dinner.

The Orthodox Church has always emphasized the home as the center of worship and religious education. The family icon and votive light are to be a constant reminder of "the church in the home" (Romans 16:5).

Setting aside one specific evening each week as a FAMILY HOME EVENING is a very effective way of solidifying the family and *making* time for important family activities such as praying together, singing together, discussing family problems together, playing together, reading the Bible together, etc.

For example, when problems arise or a decision must be made, large or small, it can be discussed during the family home evening. We can ask the question, "What do you think the Lord Jesus would want us to do in such a situation?" We can proceed from there, letting each person express what he or she thinks Christ would want us to do.

Every Orthodox Christian family should have a weekly family home evening. It is an excellent way to create a unified, Christ-centered family. We need to remember that each home is a *religious* institution; parenthood is a *holy calling*, a priesthood.

When the Sunday school was founded several years ago, it was intended for children who had either no parents or ungodly parents. They were taken off the streets on Sunday to be taught at school what they should have been taught at home. The Sunday school was not founded for children who had a good Christian home. *Christian parents taught their children at home.* They taught them so much that they did not feel any need for an organized school on Sunday. The best school for them on Sunday was to participate as a family in the divine liturgy. How this has changed! In most cases today we have turned the spiritual education of our children over to a church school teacher who tries to do in less than one hour on Sunday what the parents should be doing all week long.

It is time for Orthodox Christian families to revive "the church in the home." A special weekly family home evening will be a great help in achieving this. Many of the exercises in this book are designed for use during the family home evening.

Creating a Faith Atmosphere At Home

The first level of faith is called *experiential*. It is the level of childhood faith where children experience faith through those around them. Children cannot understand theology, doctrine or catechism at this stage, but they can understand God through the daily faith experiences, the rituals, the symbols, and traditions of those near and dear to them. What the family does at home, the simplest of evening blessings, or a spontaneous prayer around the family table, is more basic to life-long faith than most of us realize.

Parents need to work hard at creating such a "faith" atmosphere at home. God becomes a living God when our relationship to Him becomes personal. As Nikos Kazantzakis put it: "Wherever you find husband and wife, that's where you find God; wherever children and petty cares and cooking and arguments and reconciliation are, that is where God is too." The God of the incarnation is perhaps more domestic than monastic. Let me share with you how an Orthodox Christian from Greece describes this "faith" atmosphere-the experiential stage-as it existed in his childhood years:

I am still yearning for the small village church, the long candlelight procession on Good Friday evening, and the outdoor midnight celebration of the Resurrection (the Anastasis as we call it in Greek), with fireworks and great exuberance. Holy Week in Greece has a much stronger family flavor. There is fasting throughout the week and a lot of preparations at home (baking tsourekia), dyeing red eggs, making the special mageritsa soup, roasting a lamb on a

spit, etc. for the celebration of the Anastasis.
Practically every member of the family works hard in
these preparations so that Easter is finally celebrat-
ed in a joyous family atmosphere. It is like
Christmas here in America, but even more so.

A Halakah or Way of Life

This way of life is called *halakah* in Hebrew. Judaism
was above all a *halakah*, a way of life. Being a Jew meant
that you were different. It had an effect on what you ate, how
you dressed, how you spent your Friday night, how far you
walked on the Sabbath day, etc. Being a Jew permeated your
whole life. It meant praying four times a day. It meant teaching your faith to your children.

Harvard sociologist, Harvey Cox, said, "The family
needs an entirely new lifestyle if it is to survive." We
Orthodox Christians have always had such a *halakah*,
lifestyle for the family. Our problem is that for various reasons we have ignored it. It is this Orthodox Christian
lifestyle for the family that is offered in the book you are now
reading. Our purpose through the use of the family exercises that you will find in this book is to help create a strong and
nurturing "faith" atmosphere at home not for just one week
or season but throughout the whole year by latching on to the
liturgical cycle of the church year. There are many practical
ways by which we can accomplish this and at the same time
establish some powerful Christian family traditions for the
home.

What to Do on the Way to and From the Liturgy

An Orthodox Christian family can make excellent use of the time they drive to and from church. It is one of those rare times when the whole family is together. Since parents are the primary and most effective priests and religious educators their children will ever have, they can use this time to talk about the sermon. Ask the children to state in their own words what they learned from the sermon. As they answer, ask them more questions about it. This will teach the children that the parents consider listening to God's word important. It will also teach them to listen carefully.

Once the sermon is covered, the parents can begin to ask each child what was learned in the Sunday school class. Here again, the child will be motivated to listen in the classroom knowing that the parents will be interested in knowing what was taught. Parents have the distinct advantage of knowing most of the experiences of their children. They know best, therefore, how to relate and explain to their children certain things that were said in church and Sunday school. If parents are interested in what their children are learning, the children will realize the importance of God and the church in their lives. They will also be more likely to ask questions about something they do not understand.

One mother has learned to boil each Sunday's sermon down to one short statement which she then attaches to the refrigerator. She writes, "Since I pass the refrigerator a dozen times a day, and everyone else uses it, it seemed like a perfect spot . . . . At first my children joked about my refrigerator sermons, but they were always eager to see what the sign would say each Sunday afternoon . . . it has also provided my husband and me with a helpful basis for continuing our children's church education at home." If we cannot summarize each Sunday's sermon into one short statement, we can always substitute a Bible verse we have read.

Thus, the time commuting to and from church may be used constructively. One family takes a Bible story book along that has lots of pictures. They read a story-whichever the children choose-and sometimes two-on the way to church. "Before this," says one parent, "the boys aged three to nine, usually argued and fought all the way." If the children are older, they can take turns reading aloud the pre-Communion prayers on the way to church. The way to and from church need not be wasted; it is precious time that can be used to make God more real to our children.

On Keeping Epiphany the Year Round

One of the major holy days on the calendar of the Orthodox Church is Epiphany or Theophany, which is celebrated on January 6 (thirteen days later in Orthodox churches which observe the Julian calendar). In order to help their children understand this beautiful service and participate in it meaningfully, parents can talk about it at home a few days beforehand. Following is a brief explanation they can use.

On January 6 we celebrate the great feast of Epiphany. Derived from the Greek, the word "epiphany" means "the showing forth" or "the manifestation." It was on this day that Christ was made known as the Son of God. It was on this day that our Lord appeared before John the Baptist in the River Jordan and asked to be baptized-not that He was sinful and needed to be cleansed through baptism, but that He might teach us the importance and necessity of this great sacrament. While He was being baptized, the Holy Spirit descended upon Him in the form of a dove and the voice of the Father was heard from heaven saying, "*This is my beloved Son, with Whom I am well pleased.*" Thus on this day not only does heaven tell us that Christ is God, but we see God manifested in the Holy Trinity. We have before us the three persons of the Godhead: the Son, being baptized in the River Jordan; the Holy Spirit in the form of a dove, and the voice of the Father in Heaven: Father, Son and Holy Spirit. This is the meaning of the great feast of Epiphany-the showing forth or manifestation of God in three Persons.

A few days ago (Christmas) we saw Christ as a new-born babe. Today (Epiphany) we see Him a full-grown man of 30 beginning His public ministry among people. Today the Little Entrance of the Divine Liturgy is expanded into a full celebration. It is in this procession of coming forth from the Holy Altar and carrying the Gospel aloft, that the priest represents Jesus Christ coming forth to bring the Gospel of salvation to all. The Little Entrance of the Divine Liturgy is in reality a little Epiphany.

On this great feast of the Epiphany, the Church of Christ calls all of us to go together to the River Jordan to witness the manifestation of God and the Baptism of our Lord Jesus Christ. There we shall see, with the eyes of our soul, our Lord immersing Himself once again in the waters of the River Jordan, and thus sanctifying the oceans and the rivers and the lakes of the world.

At the conclusion of the liturgy on Epiphany the priest will perform the special Rite of the Blessing of the Waters. He will ask our Lord that just as 2,000 years ago He blessed the water in the Jordan River, so today He bless the water that we have before us so that in the words of the prayer: "*those who pour and partake thereof (of the Holy Water) may receive it for the cleansing of souls and bodies, for the healing of suffering, for the sanctification of homes, and for every need.*" Upon leaving church we shall all take a bottle of this holy water home with us to bless ourselves and our homes. "Today the streams of Jordan are changed into healing waters by the presence of the Lord," says the prayer of Patriarch Sophronius of Jerusalem, recited in the Rite of the Blessing of Water in Epiphany.

In some parts of the country an Orthodox bishop casts a cross into a body of water to be retrieved by a swimmer. In the local parish the priest will immerse a cross into a vessel containing water. This act represents our Lord immersing Himself once again in the River Jordan and sanctifying all the oceans, rivers and lakes of the world. Thus the water becomes blessed, or holy, and brings to us the healing presence of the Lord.

Children should be encouraged to keep the small bottle of holy water which they will receive on this day. They can place it by their icon and use it the year round. They can use it to bless themselves or their room or their new bicycle, etc. They can partake of it with a spoon when they feel they have a special need for the Lord's presence at home. It will represent the Lord's healing and loving presence with them constantly as does the family icon. Thus we can teach them to keep Epiphany the year round.

A Prayer Line

A housewife found a new way of praying one day while ironing. She got to thinking about how many lines there were-bus lines, telephone lines, clothes lines, fishing lines. "Why not a prayer line?" she asked. So she strung up a short rope across one corner of her kitchen. On it she hung cards with the names of shut-ins, of the sick, of the bereaved. As she ironed she prayed for these people by name.

This gives us an idea. Why not string such a line beneath the family icon? Or if the icon sits on a table, why not take pieces of paper, fold then in half, and stand then on the table around the icon? Encourage the members of your family to keep adding to these names as they think of persons who need to be remembered before the throne of God's grace. This gesture places these persons close to Christ (the icon) and makes it easy for us to remember them in prayer.

Praying for others is called intercessory prayer. It is an expression of love. We care enough for others to share their burdens by praying for them. As the four friends brought the paralytic to Jesus and placed him before the Master's feet for healing, so we can bring others to Jesus today and place them before Him for healing and strength.

One person takes the newspaper with him every night when he prays. He reads the birth notices and prays for the new babies and the families. He reads wedding announcements and prays for the couples who are to be married. He reads the deaths in the obituary column and prays that God's comfort may come to those who have lost loved ones. There is no end to the number of persons we can bring to the throne of God's grace through intercessory prayer.

The great litany at the very beginning of the liturgy is a

good example of intercessory prayer. It is an all-embracing prayer showing the church's concern for everyone and everything in the universe.

Frank C. Laubach has written, "Most of us will never enter the White House and offer advice to the President. Probably he will never have time to read our letters. But we can give him what is far more important than advice. We can give him a lift into the presence of God, make him hungry for divine wisdom, which is the grandest thing one can ever do for another. We can visit the White House with prayer *as many times a day as we think of it,* and every such visit makes us a channel between God and the President."* Truly, there is no place intercessory prayer cannot reach, no door it cannot open. Let it become part of our daily prayer life at home through a visible "prayer" line.

---

* "Prayer the Mightiest Force in the World" by Frank C. Laubach, Spire Books.

The Parental Blessing

One father practices the Old Testament custom of blessing each child every evening before retiring for sleep. He makes the sign of the cross on each child's forehead and says, "May the blessing of God the Father, the Son, and the Holy Spirit be with you John/Jane tonight and forevermore." He then kisses each child. This can also be done in the morning by mom or dad before children leave for school as well as before bedtime. Grandparents can also join in the blessing. Have the children jump into your lap, give them a hug, read them a story and give them a generous blessing. At times you may wish to rock your child to sleep, as you slowly and softly sing your blessing. Imagine what such a blessing does to a child, what peace, what love it imparts: how real it makes the presence and love of God.

To this very day, every Friday night finds a Jewish father calling his entire family together for a time of blessing. One Christian person describes what he experienced in a Jewish home:

In Orthodox Jewish homes, blessing children is also interlaced with words that picture a special future. I saw this blessing in a Jewish home I was invited to visit one Thanksgiving. By the time I arrived, almost forty people were preparing or waiting patiently for a scrumptious dinner. With the grandparents, parents, and their children, three generations had assembled for this special occasion.

When the meal was prepared and before it could be served, the patriarch of the family (the grandfather in this case) gathered all the family together. He had all the men and their sons stand on one side of the living room, and all the women and their daughters stand on the other side. He went around, placing his hands on the head of every person in the room saying to each man, "May God richly bless you, and may He make you as Ephraim and Manasseh," and to each woman, "May God richly bless you, and may you grow to be like Rebekah and Sarah."

Such a blessing of parents for children can be traced back to the early Church where it was customary for parents to bless children. It is a tradition we need to re-claim.

The Feast of the Presentation: Time for Commitment

Every year the Orthodox Church celebrates the Presentation of Jesus in the Temple on February 2.

The Scriptural account of this event is found in St. Luke 2:22. We suggest that this be read to the children by one of the parents.

The day on which Jesus was brought to the Temple and presented to God (dedicated), 40 days after His birth, is time for us to be reminded that our parents did the same with us 40 days after our birth. They brought us to Church and presented us to the Lord. The priest took us into his arms and brought us before the altar offering prayers in our behalf.

When we were baptized, we were again presented to the Lord for cleansing and adoption. At both times it was others who brought us to Christ because of our infancy. Others confessed the Nicene Creed for us. Others made the profession of faith for us.

Since we cannot enter heaven on another's faith, it is time to make our own commitment to Christ. What better time for this than on the anniversary of Christ's dedication to God: the Feast of the Presentation?

Life is Commitment

Sooner or later every person must give himself to something bigger than himself. We will submit to some master in life whether that master be work, having a good time, making a lot of money, etc.

Our great problem is to choose which master we will serve. The only true Master Who is worth serving is the Lord

Jesus Christ. He alone is God. He alone can help us find happiness and purpose in life.

Often when people are asked why they are members of the Orthodox Church, they say, "I guess I was born into it. I guess it just runs in the family."

At this point, ask the children: Have you ever thought about why you are an Orthodox Christian? Are you one just because you were born into it? Encourage them to share their views.

The real reason why anyone is a true Orthodox Christian is that one has committed or given one's life completely to Jesus Christ as Lord and Master, as Son of the Living God. This happens within the Orthodox Church which is the body through which Christ continues to be present in the world today.

If you have never given your life to Jesus as Lord, then nothing in the world can make you an Orthodox Christian. If Orthodox Christianity is anything, it is commitment to Jesus as Lord. "Jesus is Lord," was one of the first creeds of the early Christians.

When we were baptized, Jesus said to each one of us, "Yes, I accept you as my son or daughter. I will stand by you. I will never leave you. I will come to live within you. One day I will lead you to heaven." There must come a time in our lives when we must say to Jesus, "Yes, Jesus, I thank You for what You did for me in baptism. I accept You as my God, my Lord, my King, and I give my life to You completely."

Committing one's life to anything less than Christ is like wanting to cross the Atlantic Ocean in a carton box instead of an ocean liner or a jet plane. Committing one's life to Christ is like giving yourself to the strongest Person in the universe.

At this point try the following experiment. Have a child

(or the parent) button a coat or jacket placing the second button in the first hole. Then do it the right way: first hole in the first button.

When we place first things first in life everything else falls in its proper place (first button in first hole). When we place second or third things in first place, nothing comes out right. Placing first things first is to place Christ first in our lives as Lord. When we do this, He will help us with all the other decisions we have to make in life, i.e., choosing the right partner in marriage, our goals, our life work, etc.

If we do not give our life to Christ, then we will fall for anything that comes along. We will become slaves to alcohol or money or drugs, etc. These are false masters who will make us slaves.

One true Christian said once, "I could not drift along as I had been doing, going to church because I had always gone. Either Christ was God, and Savior, and Lord, or He wasn't. If He was, then He had to have all my time, all my devotion, all my life."

Suggestion: You may have the children kneel before the family icon and celebrate the brief service below from the first part of the Sacrament of Baptism. Parent to children:

1. Do you renounce the devil and all of his works?
2. Do you accept Christ as your Lord and Savior?
3. Do you commit your life to Him as Lord?
4. Make a confession of faith by reciting the Nicene Creed.
5. A short personal prayer of commitment and thanksgiving may be offered at this point.

Come! Greet the Risen Lord in the Sunday Matins

Take your children to the Matins service some Sunday morning and see enacted before you one of the most meaningful services you will ever see.

Before you do so, explain the meaning of what they will see as follows.

During the Matins a Gospel lesson is read. There is a cycle of eleven such Gospel readings each of which tells the story of one of the post-resurrection appearances of the Risen Lord. A different Gospel lesson is read each Sunday morning until the entire eleven are completed; then the series starts again from the beginning. The Gospel readings are called the morning (eothina) Gospel lessons. The word "morning" is used not only because these lessons are read early in the morning, but also because they each tell of the Resurrection which took place early in the morning. The significance of the number eleven is twofold. It refers to the eleven apostles to whom the Resurrected Lord appeared as well as to the eleven times Jesus appeared to His disciples following the Resurrection.

During and following the reading we witness an actual re-enactment of the Resurrection of the Lord. Dressed as an angel in white vestments, the priest reads the Gospel lesson proclaiming the glorious resurrection. He reads the lesson not from the pulpit but from the right side of the altar which represents the tomb of Jesus, i.e., the exact spot where the angel stood when he first announced the Resurrection to the myrrh-bearing women who came early in the morning to anoint His body.

The re-enactment continues. Through the eyes of faith

the people of God have witnessed the Resurrection as told in the Gospel lesson. They now come forward to reverence the Risen Lord. The priest carries the Gospel book, one side of which is engraved with the Risen Lord, out of the altar to the people. This procession represents Christ walking out of the tomb and standing in the midst of His people, as He stood in the midst of His disciples. Like the myrrh-bearing women and the disciples, we too come forward to offer Him the kiss of our love and commitment. Like them we may now proclaim to the world, "We have seen the Lord, the One Who rose from the dead to destroy death by His death; the One Who is in our midst even now to resurrect us from the tombs of death in which we imprison ourselves; the One Who comes to give us now the peace of God's forgiveness."

Properly explained, this service will show our children the reality and the power of the Risen Lord Who not only appeared to His disciples following the Resurrection but Who also comes to us today. We can touch Him. We can hear Him. We can kiss Him. We can receive power from Him.

The beautiful and inspiring services of the Orthodox Church are like audio-visual aids that can assist the Orthodox home to teach effectively and dramatically some of the most basic teachings of our faith.

Teaching Our Children to Pray the Daily Hours

We can learn to practice an excellent system of daily meditation from the Orthodox cycle of daily worship.

The New Testament follows a system of telling time according to which the first hour of the day is hour one after sunrise or 7 a.m. Hour two is 8 a.m. Hour three is 9 a.m., etc.

Using this time schedule the early Christians would pause for prayer and meditation every third hour during the day. For example, we know that the apostles Peter and John "went up together into the temple at the hour of prayer, *being the ninth hour*" (Acts 3:1). We find St. Peter praying on Simon's housetop "at the sixth hour" (Acts 10:9).

The monastic orders devised prayer services for common worship around the system of "hours." Their life became a constant balance between prayer and work. They would enter the sanctuary for prayer at the third hour (9 a.m.), the sixth hour (noon), the ninth hour (3 p.m.) and the twelfth (6 p.m.). They paused for prayer in the morning, noon, afternoon and evening. We still celebrate "the service of the hours" in the Orthodox parish every Holy Friday, Christmas, and Epiphany. This New Testament way of telling time is still in use today in the monasteries of Mt. Athos.

Each of the four hourly cycles of prayer had a special theme which related to something in the history of salvation that happened at that hour. The worship service composed by the Church Fathers for that hour usually included scripture readings, psalms and hymns relating to that event.

We shall examine each hour with the special purpose of teaching our children to pause briefly on these hours each day to meditate and pray.*

The First Hour

The first hour (hour one after the rise of the sun or 7 a.m.), has as its central theme the coming of the light in the dawn of a new day. The coming of the physical light reminds the Christian of the coming of Him Who is the Light of the World. The physical light is but an icon or image of Christ. Thus, the Christian begins the day by praising God for the dawn of the physical light as well as for the Light of the World which shines brightly in the face of Jesus. We pray that His light will guide us and show us the way for the day, blessing also the works of our hands which begin daily at this hour.

The Third Hour

The third hour (three hours after sunrise or 9 a.m.), was the exact time the Holy Spirit descended upon the apostles on the day of Pentecost (Acts 2:15). This single theme dominates the third hour. One of the three psalms that are read is the 51st which contains petitions for the sending of the Holy Spirit: "Create in me a clean heart, O God; and renew a right spirit within me . . . take not thy holy spirit from me . . . and uphold me with thy free spirit" (Ps. 51:10-12).

Special prayers are said to thank God for sending the Holy Spirit on Pentecost, beseeching Him to bestow the gift

---

* A helpful booklet for those who wish to pray the Hours is "A Manual of the Hours of the Orthodox Church." Available through Light and Life Publ. Company, Minneapolis, MN. 55416

of the Spirit's presence upon us for the works of that day. The third hour is a daily reminder that the life of the faithful Christian remains empty without the inner presence of the Spirit. He is the One Who provides inner peace and power. He is the One "in Whom we live and move and have our being" (Acts 17:28).

The Sixth Hour

The sixth hour, six hours following sunrise (noon), coincides with the hour the Lord Jesus was crucified (Matt. 27:45, Luke 23:44, John 19:14). Each day at noon the Church tries to focus our attention on this great event in the history of our salvation. We offer Him prayers of gratitude for so loving each one of us that He gave His only begotten Son so that we who believe in Him may not perish but have life everlasting (John 3:16). Our noontime prayers (sixth hour) include petitions that He save us from the sins and temptations of that day.

The Ninth Hour

The ninth hour, nine hours following sunrise (3 p.m.), is the time when Jesus died on the cross. "And at about the *ninth hour* Jesus cried with a loud voice, saying, 'Eli, Eli, lama sabachthani?' That is to say, 'My God, my God, why hast thou forsaken me?' . . . When he had cried again with a loud voice, (Jesus) yielded up the ghost" (Matthew 27:46, 50). At this time prayers of thanksgiving are offered to Him Who by His death destroyed death. The prayers of the ninth hour conclude with a petition that we put to death the old sinful nature within us to enable us to live the new life in Christ

Jesus with Whom we were not only crucified but also resurrected through baptism.

Praying the Hours Today

The service of the hours was not able to survive outside the monastic environment. People simply did not have the time to flock to the monasteries three or four times a day. Yet how much we need the inspiration and the power that comes to us today from the prayerful observance of these hours.

It is for this reason we suggest that in every Orthodox home parents teach their children the meaning of the daily hours of prayer, encouraging them to pause briefly and prayerfully each day at:

the FIRST HOUR, 7 a.m., to thank Jesus for the physical and spiritual light as a new day dawns;

the THIRD HOUR, 9 a.m., the hour of Pentecost, to thank God for the Holy Spirit beseeching Him for the Spirit's presence with us throughout that day;

the SIXTH HOUR, noon, to pause at that, the moment of His crucifixion, to thank Him for His great love for us;

the NINTH HOUR, 3 p.m., to remember Him Who expired in our behalf at that very hour, repeating the words of the dying thief: "Remember me, Lord, when you come into your kingdom."

the TWELFTH HOUR, 6 p.m., we pause as darkness comes to remember Him Who came to be "a light for revelation to the Gentiles."

the COMPLINE, 9 p.m., after supper and before retiring;

the MIDNIGHT HOUR, to remember Him Who will

come again as "a thief in the night" to judge the living and the dead.

The prophet David refers to these seven daily hours of prayer when he writes:
"Seven times a day I have praised you" (Psalm 119:164). And he mentions the midnight hour of prayer: "At midnight I will rise to give thanks to You" (Psalm 119:62).

Teach Them the Orthodox Rule of Prayer

The Orthodox Church has given us what is known as a Rule of Prayer. This is a period of time that is set aside each day for prayer. The reason for such a rule of prayer is that "you cannot wait to be in the mood; you have to use the spur of your Prayer Rule to force yourself to pray."*

Our Orthodox tradition also provides a basic outline of content for the Rule of Prayer which begins with a simple invocation of the name of God, i.e., we make the sign of the cross and say, "In the Name of the Father and of the Son and of the Holy Spirit. Amen." This is followed by the prayer to the Holy Spirit, "O Heavenly King . . ." which is followed in turn by the Trisagion Prayers. Of course, this is only the beginning of the Rule of Prayer. It may go on to include the reading of a psalm, a Scripture reading, the Nicene Creed, some of the petitions from the liturgy, a period of silence, special petitions of praise and thanksgiving, intercessions for other people, etc. It can be as long or as short as one pleases. It depends on each person. Remember that the prayer of the thief on the Cross was very short, "Lord, remember me in your kingdom;" and the prayer of the Publican was equally short, "Lord, be merciful to me, the sinner."

So if you have not already started, begin to form a daily Rule of Prayer. Use the Trisagion prayers of the Church as the foundation upon which to build. Begin humbly and simply-but begin. You will be greatly blessed.

Someone said, "Heaven must be full of answers to

* "Light in the Darkness" by Sergi Fudel. SVS Press. Crestview, NY. 1989

prayers for which no one ever bothered to ask."

Fr. Charles Bell tells how the Rule of Prayer helped him in his daily prayer life:

> *One of the advantages I have found in using a rule of prayer is that it takes away the burden of needing to be creatively new teach time I pray. On many occasions I do not feel creative or particularly inspired. At such times, the temptation is to cease praying altogether, until such time as the inspiration returns. This usually means that the habit of prayer is broken, or rather, never really established. However, in Orthodox spirituality, one follows the assigned rule of prayer, "in season and out of season." I am not forced to rely on my own creativity or spontaneity, but rather can rely upon Spirit inspired prayers of Christ's Church. This means that even in spiritually dry times, I can continue with the habit of prayer because a tried and tested structure or rule of prayer has been provided for me by my spiritual Father. Thus I'm enabled to continue the habit of prayer in both spiritually rich and dry times, eventually such perseverance produces, by God's grace, the virtue of a life of prayer."* *

An Orthodox Rule of Prayer
In the name of the Father, the Son, and the Holy Spirit. Amen.
Glory to You, our God, glory to you.
God, have mercy on me, the sinner!

---

* "Discovering the Rich Heritage of Orthodoxy." Fr. Charles Bell, Ph.D. Light and Life Publishing Company. Minneapolis, MN. 2001

A Prayer to the Holy Spirit

Heavenly King, the Comforter, the Spirit of truth, present everywhere and filling all things, treasury of blessings and giver of life, come and abide in us. Cleanse us from every stain and save our souls, gracious Lord.

The Thrice-Holy Hymn

Holy God, Holy Mighty, Holy and Immortal, have mercy on us. (3 times) Glory to the Father, the Son and the Holy Spirit, now, forever, and to the ages of ages. Amen.

A Prayer to the Holy Trinity

All Holy Trinity, have mercy on us. Lord, cleanse us from our sins. Master, forgive us when we disobey You. Holy One, come to us and heal our weaknesses for the sake of Your Name.
Lord have mercy. (3 times)
Glory to the Father, the Son, and the Holy Spirit, now, forever, and to the ages of ages. Amen.

The Lord's Prayer

Our Father who art in heaven, hallowed be Thy name. Thy kingdom come. Thy will be done on earth as it is in heaven. Give us this day our daily bread. Forgive us our trespasses as we forgive those who trespass against us. Lead us not into temptation but deliver us from evil. Amen.

Have Your New Home Blessed

It is a wonderful Orthodox Christian practice to invite the priest to bless your new apartment or home. This can be done either before you move in or after you are settled.

The priest will conduct a brief prayer service after which he will bless each person in your family and each room of your home with holy water.

We read in Revelation 3:20, "Behold, I stand at the door and knock; if any one hears my voice and opens the door, I will come in to him, and eat with him, and he with me." This is a beautiful picture of what Christ wants to do when we move into a new home or apartment. He wants us to open the door to let Him come in to bless us. He wants to stay and fellowship with us in a very intimate way as expressed through eating and the drinking together.

This is what we do when we invite the priest to bless us and our new home: we open the door to let Jesus come in. If we have a new icon for our home, we shall give it to the priest at church for the formal blessing. He will bring it with him to install it in its proper place in your home and light the votive light before it for the first time.

In addition to the blessing received, such a home visit by the priest will afford your children an excellent opportunity to get to know the parish priest as a dear and personal friend in Christ. It will also teach them that Orthodox Christians seek God's blessing before every important venture in life.

I shall never forget the testimony of a friend, "When I was a very small child, a priest visited in our home. His presence was so impressive that today, 45 years later, I can still describe where he sat. I do not remember the words he spoke, but I remember his presence. Our family must have been very important for him to visit us. At least, I felt very important."

The Old Testament Mezuzah

In the Old Testament, when a family moved into a new home, there would take place a religious ceremony of dedication. The head of the household would nail a "mezuzah" on the doorpost of the house and recite a "Bracha," a blessing: "Blessed art Thou, O Lord, who hast hallowed us by Thy commandments and commanded us to affix the mezuzah." What is a *mezuzah*? And what is the biblical command, Deut. 6:9 and 11:20, "And thou shalt write them upon the doorposts of thy house and upon thy gates?" A *mezuzah* is a small metal or wooden case which contains a small parchment scroll on which is inscribed in Hebrew the affirmation of faith and love in God-the *Shema*, "Hear O Israel, the Lord is our God, the Lord is one. And you shall love the Lord your God . . ." The *mezuzah* is a constant reminder to everyone who comes to the house that it is a home where the Divine Presence dwells; that it is a home dedicated to God. It is the symbol of God's watchful care over the dwellers "from the rising of the sun to its setting" (Psalm 113:3). To this day one finds this widely observed ceremonial commandment amongst Jews. The custom is to touch or kiss the *mezuzah* upon entering and leaving the home. It is thus the remembrance of a covenant between the household and God.

The Christian Mezuzah: The Icon

When an Orthodox Christian family moves into a new

home, the normal practice is to invite the priest to bless the new house and to install and bless officially the family icon-the Christian *mezuzah*: from that moment on the family icon will serve as "God's presence" in that home. In fact, in old Russia the icon was placed by the front door. A guest, upon entering, would first reverence the icon, and then turn to greet the host.

A story is told of a young person who was just married. His father visited the home the newlyweds had just furnished and decorated. After they had shown him the place with pride and satisfaction, the father remarked, "Yes, it's very nice, but no one walking through here would know whether you belong to God or the devil!" The son was shocked by his father's gruff but well-meaning comment. But he got the point. From that day forward, he made certain that in every room of his home there was some evidence of their faith in Christ. What better evidence than an icon on the wall, a Bible on the table and a family prayer corner!

One of the most indelible memories of childhood for many is the annual visit of the priest at Epiphany. The family leads the priest all through the house, from room to room, holding candles and the icon of the feast as he sprinkles the walls and the furniture with holy water, as all sing the Troparion of Theophany:

> *When You, O Lord, were baptized in the Jordan, the worship of the Trinity was made manifest. For the voice of the Father bore witness to You and called You His beloved Son. And the Spirit in the form of a dove confirmed the truthfulness of His word. O Christ our God, who has revealed yourself and has enlightened the world, glory to You!*

The Family Table

It has been said that the most important piece of furniture in the house is the family table. Edmund Barbotin calls it, ". . . the social furnishing. It is . . . made for reunions. Being accessible from all sides the table is made to be surrounded . . . It is here that the family, daily scattered is daily reunited." However well or poorly made, the table is the family's treasure. Gathered at table, every meal is called to be a communion in its sharing of food, in our conversation, in our prayer. The great religious festivals of the Old Testament were celebrated, and are still celebrated today by our Jewish brethren, *around the family table.* We often forget that we Orthodox Christians come out of the Old Testament. Our roots are there.

We need to reclaim the practice of celebrating the great festivals of the Church year in our home *around the family table.* This is how they become real and indelible to our children. St. John Chrysostom in a sermon instructed husbands in the procedure of the family meal: "After eating they are to stand up with their wives and children and sing hymns together. The whole proceedings are to conclude with a prayer . . . ." Some families place a small icon of Jesus on the dinner table, with a votive light before it. The children take turns lighting the candle. They hold hands together as dad offers the prayer. After dinner they have a devotion and discussion. They talk about what they believe. They share their Christian values. The read God's word together. They tell stories. They share what happened during the day. And they conclude with prayer. Dr. Lee Salk, a noted child psychologist, wrote,

Mealtime is incredibly important. People used to talk and listen at mealtime, but now they sit in front of their television set with their TV dinner. I don't care how busy you are-you can take that time with your children. You can talk about your dreams; you can talk about your day; you can talk about your frustrations. The busier you are, the more valuable mealtime is for your child. If we don't spend this time with our youngsters, they are not going to develop healthy attitudes toward family life.

The Liturgy of the Family Around the Table

What takes place around the family table at mealtime may be described as the "liturgy" of the family. It begins and ends with prayer. Following the meal there can be a reading from the Bible or from devotional literature or the lives of the saints. We need to see the family meal as a place for true learning, sharing and praying. For some it is the only time when the entire family is assembled together. Here the child can interact with adults; learn the art of conversation, both speaking and listening; find out what is going on in the lives of brothers, sisters, parents; celebrate in big and little ways the events of family and religious life such as birthdays, exams passed , first jobs, merit badges, major holy days, a new tooth, a promotion, and all other events that mean more when we share them with the people closest to us.

One parent said, "At mealtimes we each take a turn and say one thing that we are grateful for, that happened to us that day." As such, the family meal is an ideal time for family togetherness, prayer, and devotions. Thus one of the truly great things in family life are the meals, the *koinonia*, and fellowship we share together. A shared meal with the whole family *around the family table* is what may be called a family sacrament, a means of grace, uniting the family to God and to each other. One person wrote,

> *Eating has always been important to me, because the focal point of the day is the dinner table, a foretaste of the heavenly banquet. The dinner hour is a sacramental time for me, a time of gratitude for whoever is gathered around the table, for the food, for our being part of the great story of Creation. We share the day's events, tell stories, look up words in dictionaries, linger long after the meal is over while the candles burn down.*

The family table can be an important altar where meals are celebrated, stories of our faith are shared, personal histories are recounted and where parents fulfill their priestly roles.

Prayers at the Table

Before Meals
O Christ our God, bless the food and drink of Thy servants, for Thou art Holy, now and ever. Amen.

After Meals
Blessed art Thou, O Christ our God, Who ever feeds us from the bounteous gifts by Thy grace. Thou has satisfied us with Thy earthly gifts; deprive us not of

Thy Heavenly Kingdom; but as Thou did enter into the midst of Thy disciples, O Savior, and gave them peace, enter also among us and save us. Amen.

Tell Them About the Lives of the Saints and the Major Feast Days

The saints are the heroes of our faith. Young people need heroes-people they can look up to for inspiration and emulation. Most Orthodox Christians are named after saints. The purpose of naming Christians after saints is to give them a great name to live up to. When Alexander the Great discovered once that a soldier who bore his name had acted cowardly in battle, he charged him to change either his name or his behavior. No one who bore the name Alexander acted cowardly.

Orthodox parents can acquaint their children with the lives of the great heroes of our faith by practicing the following discipline. Consult the church calendar which gives the name(s) of the saint(s) who will be commemorated on the following day. Let us use as an example St. Nicholas who is celebrated on December 6.

On the evening of the fifth consult a book on the lives of the saints, i.e., *The Lives of the Saints and Major Feast Days* by Fr. George Poulos.* Share the life story of the saint with your children. If one of your children is named Nicholas and is old enough, he may be assigned the task of reading the life of St. Nicholas and sharing it with the members of the family. Following this, the family may sing for him "Happy Name Day to You," using the same tune as "Happy birthday to you . . . ." A special name day cake or dessert may be served. The same person-Nicholas-may be assigned the privilege of lighting the votive light before the family icon for the

---

* Your Priest will be able to suggest additional books

evening. Of course, the person whose name day is being celebrated, should attend the liturgy on his/her saint's day (or on the closest Sunday) and receive our Lord through Holy Communion.

If the event being celebrated is a scriptural happening, i.e., the Transfiguration of Jesus, look up the Scriptural lessons for the liturgy of that day (Epistle and Gospel) which are listed on the church calendar. Share these readings with your children. The Gospel lesson relates the story of the event being celebrated. Talk about the event: what it means to you. Ask the children to tell what they see in the story and to share any questions they may have.

Such a family discipline will acquaint children with the living tradition of our Orthodox Christian faith. The lives of the saints and the sacred happenings of Scripture will come alive to them. They will be motivated to follow Christ, as did the saints, to live lives that will bring glory to God and blessings to mankind. This is the way to produce new Church fathers and new saints for today's world.

One educator said, "Children need heroes just as they need food." Yet what we are offering them today is junk-food heroes. Real heroes exist especially in the saints of the Church. We need to tell their stories.

Revive Storytelling

John Westerhoff, in *Bringing Up Children in Christian Faith*, presents four guidelines for sharing our faith with our children from birth through childhood:

1. We need to tell and retell the biblical story-the stories of the faith-together.
2. We need to pray together.
3. We need to listen and talk to each other. This creates family closeness.
4. We need to perform faithful acts of service and witness together.

What will be emphasized here is the importance of storytelling. Almost all ancient knowledge was passed on to us by oral tradition (paradosis), which is another word for storytelling. In my youth, we did not have church school. My mother would tell us stories of Christ and His saints at home.

The American tragedy today is that families don't talk to each other any more. They are too glued to the tube. We need to communicate. We need to tell stories, read stories, stories about family history; stories about hungry children and children who have too much; stories about our faith; stories of the Bible; stories of God's historical acts in the lives of His people, the saints. We need to become once again a story-telling people.

As the Psalmist said,

I will utter things that I have heard and known that our fathers have told us. We will not hide from our children but tell to the coming generation the glorious deeds of the Lord, and His might and the wonders which He has wrought (Ps. 78:3-4).

St. John Chrysostom wrote,

An important part of a child's education is story-telling, since good stories excite the imagination and strengthen the bond between parent and child. Stories from the Bible are preferred, and the child should repeat them often, to underscore full comprehension.

It is through the telling of stories, Bible stories, stories of Jesus and the saints, that we pass on our faith and values to our children.

One Father said,

My wife and I simply tell them stories about what happened to us when we were growing up. As parents we tend to lecture and admonish our children, teaching the conclusions we've drawn from our experiences rather than the experiences themselves. But through the ancient art of storytelling we can recreate those learning experiences. Then our children can learn, as we did, the values that our experiences taught us . . . . The place our children take within society will be tremendously influenced by the great unpublished works we tell about our own "olden days" as we tuck our young children into their beds at night.

So, the next time you get the urge to lecture your children with a wagging finger and a screwed-up face, relax, sit down with your child and say, "You know what happened to me when I was your age." You'll have an all-ears audience.

We Are Members of His Body

Read I Cor. 12:4-20.

A little girl was telling what Jesus meant to her. She concluded by quoting these comforting words of Jesus: "And I give unto them eternal life; and they shall never perish, neither shall any man pluck them out of my hand" (John 10:28). Just then a joshing, doubting friend piped up with the question, "But suppose you slip through His fingers?" Quick as a flash, she replied, "Never, never! You see, I'm one of His fingers."

This little girl had caught the meaning of the words just read from I Cor. 12:4-20. A great biblical principle had lodged in her heart; namely, that "we are members of his body, of his flesh, and of his bones" (Eph. 5:30). She knew that she had been joined inseparably to Jesus and that she belonged to Him.

When St. Symeon the New Theologian had returned from Church one day where he had received Communion, he sat down and meditated on what had happened to his body as a result of receiving Holy Communion. "These hands," he said, "these feet, these eyes, these ears, so frail, so powerless are the hands, the feet, the eyes, the ears of Christ. This body, so mean, so old is the place of the divine presence." We are not just *disconnected* hands and feet and eyes and limbs. We are *connected* as members of His Body, animated and vivified by the breath of His Spirit.

When we speak of the grace of God working through the Church, we must remember that it is not only through the Church as a whole that God is working but through each individual, each one of us. We are individually members of His Body. "Now you are Christ's body, and each of you a limb or organ of it" (I Cor. 12:27).

"We Are Your Heart"

Shortly before his death, Dr. Tom Dooley returned to the United States to raise funds for his hospital in Southeast Asia. As a physician he knew he had terminal cancer and would not live long. But his main concern was whether his medical work would continue after his death.

While he was in America, a telegram arrived from some of the medical corpsmen he had trained to be his helpers in the mission hospital. The message read:

"We need you here. But while you are gone, we are the fingers of your flesh to heal the sick. We are your ears to hear their cries of pain. We are your heart to love them."

This is what Jesus asks each of us to do. We are His hands on this earth to heal the sick, to set the prisoner free, to restore sight to the blind. We are His ears to hear their cries of pain and despair. We are His heart to love them. He has no heart or hands but ours to do His work in the world today.

God Chooses a Body

When God desired to work among us, He took to Himself a human body like ours. We call this the Incarnation: God taking on a body and living among us. With and through that body God acted during the 33 years that He lived on earth. He taught; He healed; He forgave; He offered Himself on the Cross for our salvation. Then on Ascension Day His body left the earth, and was no longer active among us.

If God intended, after the Ascension, to do any more

work among us, He must either bring that body back again (as He will do when He comes at the Last Judgment), or else He must use some other body. He has chosen to do the latter, i.e., to make use of some other body. This time it is not a physical body, like the one born of the Virgin Mary. It is instead an organism which St. Paul likens to a body when he says, "You are Christ's body." All those Christians who have been baptized; who have received the Holy Spirit; who share in the life of Christ through the Eucharist, make up the Body that is to be the instrument of Christ's work on earth. In other words, Christ lives in all of us who share His life. He continues to work and act through us who make up His new Body, the Church.

He Needs You

Is there some wrong that must be made right? How will God do it without you? Is there some fear to be allayed in a troubled heart? How will God do it without you? Is there someone who needs to be guided to a higher road? How will God lead him there without you? Is there some home shattered by hatred that needs the love of Christ? How will Christ bring that love except through you? Toward the very end of the New Testament, we read that "God will wipe away all tears from their eyes." That He will do, but He will use your words and your compassion and the gentle touch of your hand to do it. Christ needs us. For today we Christians make up the only Body through which Christ can act to bring His love and peace to the world.

Discuss as a family how each one can use the various members of one's body to serve Christ. Be specific.

Remind your children that when they were baptized each

member of the body was marked with the sign of the cross as a sign of dedication and service to Christ.

Discovering Our God-given Talents

It is important that we teach our children that all that we have, i.e., our body, our life, our possessions, our talents, etc., do not belong to us; they are loaned to us by God. He expects us to use them for His glory and for the betterment of each other.

To each one of us God has given at least one talent or special ability which He expects us to develop and use. Read the parable of the talents (Matthew 25:14-30) and discuss it with your family. Some good discussion questions are: What is a talent? How do I know what my talent is? How can I develop it? Here it may be pointed out that each person has at least one talent. Some may have more, others less, but God has not overlooked anyone. Those who develop their talent find that it increases. Those who do not develop it, lose it.

Since children are curious they will want to know what talent or talents God has given them. It can be explained that God will show them slowly, as they grow, what special talent He has given them. He will use parents, teachers and others to help point out to them what they are best suited to do. It is good to teach them to include in their daily prayers a petition to God that He help them discover and develop the special talent He has given them.

There is great danger here with parents who make unreasonable demands on their children, expecting them to achieve five-talent brilliance in life when God has endowed them with one talent. Or the parents who compare one child to the other, forgetting that no two children have the same number of talents or the same kind. The result is that the one-talent child develops the idea that it is not worthwhile to develop the talent that he does have. "Why try? I can never hope to do as well in school as my sister or make the football team like my brother." Thus the talent that the child has is oftentimes lost, and a sense of inferiority is permitted to ruin his life. The greatest of all fairytale writers-Hans Christian Anderson-got his start from a publisher who one day saw some of his writings and said, "Not bad. Keep trying. I'll help you." Here lies one of the greatest contributions of the parent to the child: to discover what talent God has given each child and to encourage the child to develop it. A beautiful poem was written about children by Miriam Dale,

I am a little child
I paint fearlessly
I hammer loudly
I build recklessly
I read imaginatively
I write originally
I sing rapturously
May men never quell my creativity
Just refine it!

God has given each one of us some unique talent or capacity which no one else in this world possesses. Each one of us has a certain way of being helpful to others, and an ability to do certain things as no other person can do them. This gives every man, woman, and child the value of uniqueness. The world would be less if we had not been born. We have added something that was not here before we came. That something is from God, and it is precious beyond all price.

Let us help our children realize that they matter greatly to God. He has entrusted them with something He gave to no other person, and the way they use it is just as important to Him as the way the most gifted men and women use the talents they possess. As Edwin Markham said,

"There is waiting a work where only your hands can avail:

And so, if you falter, a chord in the music will fail."

Sometimes we look at a great person and we say, "Isn't he a gifted individual?" Yet are we not all gifted? Even the one talent is not ours but a gift from God. These gifts are God's investment in our life. The point of the parable is that God expects a return on His investment. One day He will ask us to account for what we did with the gifts He entrusted to us.

"You have small talents," someone said to a Christian. And the Christian replied, "Yes, but I have a great God." "He who abides in me," said Jesus, "and I in him, he it is that bears much fruit."

Celebrating Our Spiritual Birthday: The Day of Baptism

An Orthodox Christian celebrates *two* birthdays: the day of his physical birth and the day of his spiritual birth. After physical birth comes the other birth-"of water and the Spirit," our spiritual birthday.

On this day Jesus adopted me as His child. He cleansed me of all sin. He came to dwell in me through the Sacrament of Holy Communion. The Holy Spirit came to pitch His tent in me. The voice of God the Father said of me: "This is my beloved son/daughter in whom I am well-pleased."

What could be a more important day than that? It is an event that should be remembered and celebrated annually. Why not turn it into a second birthday for our children and celebrate it with a birthday party and cake? Mother can bake a "Jesus Birthday Cake" and all can sing "Happy Birthday." The sponsors (godparents) and the rest of the family can be present to give birthday presents just as they do on the regular birthday. We can light the baptismal candle to remind us of the light we received from Jesus. Parents can use the occasion as an opportunity to discuss what it means to be Jesus' children, what it means to be a member of God's own family and to bear Christ's own name, i.e., CHRIST-ian.

Such a family celebration will help the child remember *who* he is and *whose* he is. It will help reclaim what is now a forgotten day and make it into the really important day that it is.

Part of the celebration of one's second birthday should also be the receiving of Holy Communion on the Sunday closest to one's spiritual birthday. For this event, the baptismal candle should be taken to Church and held while going to receive the Precious Body and Blood of Jesus.

The celebration of one's baptism is a good time to tell your child how much you love him. Parents can say, for example, "Nick, when you were baptized God said of you, 'This is my beloved son in whom I am well pleased.' Let me tell you, Nick, this is exactly how mom and dad feel about you. We love you. You are important to us. We're glad you're a member of our family. We're glad you're here. Life wouldn't be the same without you. Sometimes, Nick, we're not as sensitive and as caring as we should be as parents and we're sorry for that. Please don't think our neglect or tactlessness means you are not important to us. You are! We love you dearly." This is also a good occasion to tell children about their baptism, why their godparents were chosen, and how their names were decided. Show them pictures of the occasion. Let them see their baptismal certificates. If you don't have one, request it from the parish where they were baptized.

An Orthodox Family Talks About Fasting

Parents may share with their children the following basic facts on fasting. The Orthodox Church has always placed great emphasis on fasting. We fast on Wednesdays because on this day the decision was made to arrest Jesus. We fast on Fridays because it is the day on which Jesus was crucified. Fasting helps us remember that these are special days in the history of our salvation. Other periods of fast are during Lent, Advent (pre-Christmas fast), the first fifteen days of August, etc.

Orthodox Christians fast from meat and products derived from meat, i.e., milk, cheese, eggs, butter, etc. The purpose of such fasting is threefold: (1) it helps us concentrate more on prayer. A full stomach is not as conducive to prayer as one not so full. (2) Fasting helps strengthen our will power. By learning to say "no" to certain types of food, we shall find it easier to say "no" to temptations. (3) Fasting is a way of helping us identify with those who hunger and provide food for them. (4) Jesus fasted. He tells us in the Bible, "*When* you fast . . . ." He does not say, "*If* you fast . . . ." He expects us to fast.

An early Christian, Aristides, wrote, "If there is a poor person among the Christians and they do not have the means to help him, they fast two or three days and give the food they have saved through fasting to the hungry person."

Orthodox Christians are called upon to fast not only for reasons of self-control and prayer, but also for reasons of love: to deny ourselves something that we may share what we have saved with a needy person.

An Example

One family decided to have a meal of just rice once a week since that is the diet of millions of underprivileged in the world. Of course, the rice was fancied up a bit. It was not watered down to a thin gruel as in the underprivileged countries. When Lent was over, this same family decided to continue once every month the practice of serving only rice for dinner. The money they saved was placed in a special envelope to be given through their church to the world's hungry. They could have obtained the money by cutting out some luxury, but they felt that the rice meal helped them *identify* with those they wished to help.

A Suggested Family Prayer Service

To express the relationship between your fasting and charity you might want to try this approach to grace before meals. Use it especially on Friday.

Leader: In the name of the Father, and of the Son and of the Holy Spirit.

All: Amen.

Leader: Before sharing this food tonight let us first recall God's Presence. Let us pause a moment to praise Him for His Goodness to us. (Different family members may mention things for which they are grateful.)

Leader: God speaks to us of sharing, of caring about our many brothers and sisters in this world who are hungry, thirsty, starving, and who are waiting for our love. As we share this meal, let us think of them and pray for them together.

All: Forgive us, Father, for making our own lives comfortable while others suffer hunger and want. Bless the little which we are doing. Help and multiply it, in Your mercy to serve the needs of those unknown to us, but known and loved by You. May they, in their own way, give thanks to You, as we do, for all Your love and care. Amen.

An Orthodox Family Practice for Saturday Evening

It has been said that the divine liturgy begins when we wake up on Sunday morning and begin washing and dressing in preparation for going to church. These are the first liturgical acts. But they are not. The liturgy begins even before this. It begins on Saturday evening. It begins not only with attendance at the vesper service; it begins also with an ancient family practice suggested by St. John Chrysostom that needs to be revived today in Orthodox Christian families. It is the practice of reading and discussing at home the Scripture lessons that are to be read in the liturgy on the following morning. The Scripture references for each Sunday and major feast day are usually listed on parish calendars.

Since it is Christ Who speaks to us through the Scripture readings it is a good practice to read these lessons (Epistle and Gospel) to your family before an icon of our Lord Jesus to show that it is He Who is speaking to us. A votive light may be lit before each reading to give expression to our faith that Jesus is the light of the world and that His word is a "lamp unto my feet and a light unto my path" (Psalm 119:105). The two lessons may be read by the parents. When the children are old enough, they may be allowed to participate in the readings and to ask questions on their meaning in a family discussion.

If practiced faithfully, this family practice will make our participation in the liturgy more meaningful. We shall come to church with a greater thirst to hear the word of God and how it is interpreted to us by the priest.

We should remember that in every liturgy we commune with Christ twice. We commune with Him as the BREAD

OF LIFE through the Sacrament of Holy Communion. We commune also with Him as the WORD OF GOD when He comes to speak to us in the Scripture readings and the sermon. Just as we prepare ourselves for Holy Communion through fasting and repentance, so through this family practice, we can prepare ourselves for receiving Christ when He comes to us as the Word of God. ". . . [F]rom childhood you have been acquainted with the sacred writings which are able to instruct you for salvation through faith in Christ Jesus" (2 Timothy 3:15).

How to Listen

When a rich member of a family died, all the relatives were called together by the lawyer for the reading of the will. As the will was being read, each person listened intently, eagerly waiting to hear his or her name mentioned. One person who had difficulty hearing, brought along an old hearing horn and placed it in his ear so that he might not miss a single word.

This is a picture of how intently we should listen when God speaks in the Scriptures. Everything He says is directed personally to us. Everything He promises has our name in it. We should try to teach our children the personal love of God for each one of them by personalizing the verses we read from Scripture. For example, in John 3:16, change "God so loved the *world* . . ." to "God so loved (*my* name) so that (*my* name) who believes in Him might not perish but have life everlasting."

Prayer Before Scripture

An Orthodox Christian always prays for the guidance of the Holy Spirit before reading Scripture. Thus, before reading the Scripture lessons at home, we recommend the use of the following prayer that is prayed by the priest in every liturgy before reading the Gospel lesson:

O Merciful Master, cause the pure light of Your knowledge to shine in our hearts, and open the eyes of our mind to understand Your message of Good Tidings. Fill us with the fear of Your blessed commandments that by subduing our earthly desires we may seek a heavenly citizenship, and may do and consider all those things that are pleasing to You. For You, O Christ our God, are the source of Light to our souls and bodies, and to You we grant glory, with Your Eternal Father, and Your all-holy, righteous and life-giving Spirit, now and ever and to all ages. Amen.

The Purpose of the "Little Church": To Produce Champions for Christ

In his letter to the Romans, St. Paul says, "Greetings also to the church that meets in their house" (Romans 15:5). Even today the home is called in Greek *ekklesioula*, the "little church." It is established as such by the Sacrament of Holy Matrimony where husband and wife are literally "crowned" by God with authority and responsibility for the home, and by the Sacrament of Chrismation by which we are ordained into the royal priesthood of believers, becoming in effect priests of the "little church," the home. It takes not one but two sacraments to ordain parents to serve as "priests" in the home: Holy Matrimony and Chrismation. "Marriage is the union of man and woman that creates the little church," said St. John Chrysostom. Our purpose as parents is to create a miniature of God's Kingdom of love in our homes.

When young couples came to Fr. Yakov in the former Soviet Union to be married, he would ask them, "Can you give birth to a saint? If you are prepared to and can, then marry; if not, I shall not bless you!" Indeed, the purpose of marriage, according to St. John Chrysostom, is to produce "champions for Christ." He further defines the family as a training ground for virtues. St. Theophan clearly told parents of their responsibility to raise their children not only as Christians but as *holy* Christians.

Elder Joseph tells us that both his parents loved to go to church and they often read spiritual books, especially the Lives of the Saints. Thus they set a good example both in their personal prayer life, and in their active concern for others. Their mother also led her six children in daily prayer. On feast days, she woke them early for Matins. Elder Joseph tells how as a child he really didn't want to get up so early to go to church! But once he did, he would be so happy the rest of the day. Between Matins and the Liturgy, they would go home and she would have John read an Akathist to the Savior or to the Mother of God while she censed the whole house. It is such godly homes that produce "champions for Christ."

Family Thank-you Notes to God and Others

Pass out a piece of blank white or colored paper to the members of your family. Encourage each child to use his or her imagination in folding it and designing a THANK YOU note from it. This can be repeated for several family sessions.

For one session, encourage your children to write a THANK YOU note to the Lord Jesus listing the blessings for which each one is thankful. After this is complete, let each child share with the other family members what he/she has written. In fact, the sharing may easily be turned into a prayer of "I AM THANKFUL TO YOU FOR . . . ." Such a thank-you-note-writing session can take advantage of the Orthodox Church calendar. Children can be encouraged to write: "Lord Jesus, I thank You for what You did for me at Christmas by . . .; on Good Friday by . . .; on Easter by . . .; on Ascension Day by . . .; on Pentecost by . . ., etc.

Parents can read to the children the story of the healing of the ten lepers by Jesus. This story shows how much Jesus appreciated the one leper who returned to thank Him for the healing (St. Luke 17:12-18).

In another family session we can encourage our children to write thank-you notes to friends and relatives. These can later be mailed.

Usually the last persons we remember to send thank-you notes to are the members of our own family. Use other family sessions for the writing of thank-you notes to mom and dad, to brothers and sisters, to your priest or bishop.

Such writing sessions will encourage our children to express their feelings of gratitude to God and others. Few things build up love in life more than the expression of praise and appreciation.

Teaching Our Children to Be Good Stewards

One of the greatest lessons Orthodox Christian parents are called upon to teach their children is to be good stewards.

Christian stewardship means that Christianity has its own principle of economics. The capitalist, for example, believes that individuals should own the wealth of the world. Socialists believe that all people should own the wealth of the world and create a great commonwealth. The Christian believes that God owns the world and that man is merely the custodian, the steward of its wealth, and that everything belongs to God. "The earth is the Lord's, and the fullness thereof." When we give something to God, we're like the little boy who says to his father, "Daddy, give me some money to buy you a present."

The ancient Jews gave God the first and the best of what they had. The best of the oil, the best of the wine, and the first-fruits of their crops were set aside for God. The animals set aside for sacrifice had to be of the finest quality. God deserves our very best-not what is left over after we have spent everything on ourselves.

Because everything we have belongs to God we cannot really "give" God anything. We can only share with Him what is His in the first place. As Dag Hammarskjold wrote in his book *Markings*:

"In the last analysis, what does the word 'sacrifice' mean? Or even the word 'gift'? He who has nothing can give nothing. The gift is God's-to God."

Many of the ancient Greek coins have an owl engraved on them. The owl was there to remind people that they ought to be as wise as owls in the way they spend their money.

Wise Christian parents will ask their children to make two columns on a piece of paper. Column number 1 will be entitled WHAT ARE WE LIVING FOR? and column number 2 will be called WHAT ARE WE SPENDING FOR? We can never determine wisely what we shall spend our money for until we realize what we are living for. What we are living for will determine whether we spend more in one month for dog food than we give to God. If Jesus is really our Lord and God, it will show in what we give each week for the support of His work through the Church.

Read together Mark 12:41-44.

The widow gave all she had and Jesus praised her. She gave sacrificially. "I will not offer unto the Lord my God that which doth cost me nothing" (2 Sam. 24:24). The widow, twice-afflicted, deprived of a breadwinner, poverty-stricken, held in her hands two copper coins which make one penny. Into the temple treasury went both coins. She could have kept one for herself but she didn't. Christ's verdict was that she had given more than all the rest. "For they all contributed out of their abundance; but she out of her poverty has put in everything she had."

Secondly, we notice that our Lord was watching the people as they were placing their money into the temple treasury. "And he sat down opposite the treasury, and watched the multitude putting money into the treasury" (Mark 12:41). Perhaps we need to be reminded today that Jesus watches, that He knows what we give, that the collection plate in which we place our gift is in reality not a brass plate but the nail-scarred hands of our Lord. Jesus always sits over against the treasury-watching! So:

Give as you would if an angel

Awaited your gift at the door.
Give as you would if tomorrow
  Found you where giving is o'er.
Give as you would to the Master
  If you met His loving look.
Give as you would of your substance
  If His hand your offering took.

Read together I Corinthians 8:5.

St. Paul speaks here of the generosity of the Christians in Macedonia. Though they were poor, they gave beyond their means to help their suffering brethren in Jerusalem. Paul said that this happened because "first they gave themselves to the Lord." Here is the essence of all true giving to God: the giving of one's self. The gift without the giver is always bare and empty and perhaps even hypocritical. There are people who send a check to the church once a year but they do not participate in the life of the church. They give money but they do not give themselves. This is not *real* giving. This is not *true* giving. This is not *Christian* giving. Christian giving involves much more than writing a check. The check is really worthless unless it expresses the gift of oneself. Someone said once, "I had been giving my money to God all my life, but I had never given myself." Without the giving of oneself no gift has value.

When the offering plate was passed in church one day a little boy asked the usher to place the plate on the floor. The lad then stepped in the plate and said, "I want to give myself to God. It is all I have to give." "First they gave themselves to the Lord."

Church giving should be *proportionate* to what we earn. The important thing in Christian giving is not *how much* we give but *how much in comparison to our ability.* One dollar a week may represent 10% of income for a widow or person on pension. On the other hand, twenty dollars a week may represent not even 1% of income for someone else. The only *minimum* the Bible recognizes is the tithe, 10% of one's income.

It is important that Orthodox Christian parents teach and encourage their children to set aside for God's work a certain percentage of what they earn each week. This can be placed in their own special offering envelope and brought to church each Sunday. Parents should show interest in what their children contribute each Sunday. A parent who gives his child $1.00 for the church offering and $7.00 for a movie is imparting a sense of values.

An example of Christian giving is Alvin Dark, former Manager of the San Francisco Giants. He wrote:

"Tithing . . . giving the first tenth of my income back to God was just as unquestioned in our home as putting on my socks before my shoes. And a nickel out of every 50 cents was quite a lot when I got up every day before dawn to pedal around my paper route. But as the years went by and my income increased, I found out I could never win in this game of giving to God. He always outgave me. He gave to me physically, financially and in a dozen other ways. He gave to me a satisfying career in baseball. Actually, if I belong to Him, He owns my income, too, all of it. I have learned that tithing is just a symbol of my trust in Him."

After hearing a sermon on stewardship once, a young man said to the pastor, "That's the trouble with Christianity and the church: it's always give, give, give!"

The pastor looked at the man and said, "Sir, I want to thank you for giving me the best definition I have yet heard of Christianity." Indeed, this is the entire record of Christianity: Give! God gave His only Son. "This is my blood. . . this is my body given for you . . . The Son came . . . to give His life as a ransom for many."

"And shall I keep giving and giving again?" And the angel replied, "No, only keep giving until He stops giving to you."

The home is the place to teach our children the Christian concept of stewardship.

A woman from a distinguished American family tells how her father taught her Christian stewardship from a very young age:

My father had three little wooden boxes, like piggy banks, and I would put a dime in one for savings and a dime in another for contributions. Then I got another dime. I think I usually spent it on candy. Once a year my father and I would sit down and decide what to do with the money in the contribution box. I would read about the 100 neediest cases in the "Times" (an annual charity for the needy families supported by the New York Times). Some of the stories were so tragic I couldn't decide which family to send my money to. Father and I would talk about it and about the fact that some families might not get as much money. So I would end up sending a letter telling the "Times" to give my money to the family who needed it the most. They got half the money in the box. The other half went to the church.

What a beautiful way for parents to teach children the responsible use of God's blessings!

Teaching our Children to Cross Themselves

The Orthodox Church uses many symbols through which our faith is expressed. One of them is making the sign of the cross. The sign of the cross is perhaps one of the most profound gestures we make. It is the mystery of the Gospel in a moment. It is a simple symbol, yet in its simplicity there lies a deep profundity. It is our Orthodox Christian faith summarized in a single gesture. When we cross ourselves, we renew the covenant (agreement) we made with God at our baptism.

Let us examine this beautiful gesture for a moment. The two index fingers and the thumb of the right hand are joined together to show that we believe in: God the Father Who loves us, God the Son Who saves us, and God the Holy Spirit Who lives in us. The three fingers are joined together to show that we believe not in three Gods but in one. The remaining two fingers stand for the two natures of Christ, i.e., that He is both God and man in one and the same Person. These two fingers are brought down into the palm of the hand to show that Jesus "came down from heaven" for our salvation. This expresses the Incarnation: "the Word became flesh and dwelt among us." The act of crossing ourselves reminds us not only of the cross and the price Jesus paid to save us from sin; it is also an expression of the greatest Christian commandment, i.e., "You shall love the Lord your God with all your mind, heart, soul and strength." When touching our head, we are saying in effect, "I love You, Lord, with all my mind." When touching our shoulders, we are saying, "I love You, Lord, with all my strength." When touching our chest, we are saying, "I love You, Lord, with all my heart and soul." Other words we use when we cross ourselves are: "In the name of the Father, and of the Son and of the Holy Spirit." The Orthodox Christian always prays in the name of the Trinity.

When we usually pray, we pray to God with our mind and heart. But when we cross ourselves, we are praying to God also with our body. St. Anthony taught that the demons and their phantasms "quickly disappear especially when a person arms himself with faith and the sign of the cross."

When we were baptized the priest first made the sign of the cross on the many parts of our body. He did this to show that we belong to Christ. Just as in the old days slaves were branded with the sign of their master, and just as cattle are branded today with the symbol of their owner, so we were branded at baptism with the sign of the cross to show that we belong to Jesus. He is our Lord and God. He is the One we are to follow and obey in life. We cross ourselves to show that we belong to the Lord Jesus.

Deliver Some of Your Prayers

A poor farmer had an accident one day and broke his leg. That meant he would be laid up for a long time, unable to work. His family was large and needed help. Someone organized a prayer meeting at the church to pray for his family. While the people were praying, asking God to help the family, there was a loud knock on the door.

Someone tiptoed to the door, opening it, and there stood a young boy who said, "My dad could not attend the prayer meeting tonight, so he just sent his prayers in a wagon." And there was the wagon loaded with potatoes, meat, apples, and other produce from the farm.

This is what intercessory prayer (praying for others) is all about. Far from being an escape from involvement, it motivates us to help the person being prayed for in whatever way we can.

Sit down as a family and think of some of the persons for whom you have been praying. See if you can "deliver" some of your prayers to these folk in the form of tangible help and assistance for specific needs they may have. Perhaps a shut-in's house needs cleaning or painting, an old widow's sidewalk needs to be cleared of snow, or the lawn mowed or the leaves raked. Perhaps some lonely person recuperating from an illness needs a hot meal. Think of persons for whom you have been praying and ask your family to decide on a certain specific way by which your prayers for them may be translated into an act of love. Involve the whole family in the project. They will all experience a foretaste of heaven as a result. The marvelous feeling of satisfaction they will experience will be a tangible expression of God's "Thank you!"

Teach Them the Jesus Prayer

One of the most commonly used prayers of the Orthodox Church is the Jesus Prayer. We read about it in that classic of Russian Orthodoxy, *The Way of a Pilgrim*, which tells of an unnamed peasant who seeks out someone who will teach him how to fulfill the Biblical command to "pray without ceasing."

He wanders through Russia and Siberia with a knapsack of dried bread for food and the charity of men for shelter. He asks many church authorities and religious people, but none can teach him how to pray without ceasing. He is about to come away from his journey empty-handed when at last he meets a holy man who teaches him the Jesus Prayer: "Lord Jesus, Son of the living God, have mercy on me a sinner." From this man he learns that to pray without ceasing is "a constant, uninterrupted calling upon the divine name of Jesus during every occupation, at all times, at all places, even during sleep." He learns to repeat it as many as 12,000 times a day without effort. The Jesus Prayer becomes a constant, warming presence within him, and brings him great joy.

What is so different about the Jesus prayer?

Prayer, to the average person, is asking God for something. The Jesus Prayer is not this. It is an attempt to change the one who prays.

St. John Chrysostom tells us how this can happen:

I implore you, brethren, never to break or despise the rule of this prayer. A Christian when he eats, drinks, walks, sits, travels or does any other thing must continually cry: "Lord Jesus Christ, Son of God, have mercy upon me." So that the name of the Lord Jesus

*descending into the depths of the heart, should sub-
due the serpent ruling over the inner pastures and
bring life and salvation to the soul. He should
always live with the name of the Lord Jesus, so that
the heart swallows the Lord and the Lord the heart,
and the two become one. And again: do not
estrange your heart from God, but abide in Him, and
always guard your heart by remembering our Lord
Jesus Christ, until the name of the Lord becomes
rooted in the heart and it ceases to think anything
else.*

Another Father of the Church says,

*Continue constantly in the name of the Lord Jesus
that the heart may swallow the Lord and the Lord the
heart, and that these two may be one. However, this
is not accomplished in a single day, nor in two days,
but requires many years and much time.*

There is tremendous power in the name of Jesus. St. Paul
says: "Everyone who calls upon the name of the Lord will be
saved" (Romans 10:13). "Christ Jesus . . . humbled himself
and became obedient to death, even death on a cross.
Therefore God has highly exalted him and given him the
name that is above every name, that in the name of Jesus
every knee should bow, of things in heaven, and things on
earth and things under the earth" (Phil. 2:5-10). Jesus says in
John 14:13, "If you ask anything in my name, I will do it."
St. Peter says, "And there is salvation in no one else, for there
is no other name under heaven given among men by which
we must be saved" (Acts 4:12). The power of the Jesus

Prayer, then, lies in the name of Jesus, "the name that is above every name." Thus, the name "Jesus" alone can fulfill the whole need of the one who prays when it is prayed with faith and with a life that is lived in obedience to Christ.

Many times we wonder how the early Christian martyrs marched to their death so courageously. We cease to wonder about the stories of their courage, however, when we consider the life of St. Ignatius, the God-bearer, Bishop of Antioch, who was crowned in Rome with a martyr's death under the emperor Trajan. We read about him: "When they were taking him to be devoured by wild beasts and he had the name of Jesus constantly on his lips, the pagans asked him why he unceasingly remembered that name. The saint replied that he had the name of Jesus Christ written in his heart and that he confessed with his mouth Him whom he always carried in his heart." The Jesus Prayer gave him the power to face death victoriously.

The Jesus Prayer can give us the same power to resist every evil thought and temptation with which Satan attacks us. For example, when Satan knocks on the door of the mind seeking entrance through some evil thought, send Jesus to the door and he will flee. Resist every temptation with the Jesus Prayer. As soon as you feel that the stronghold of your soul is being assaulted by Satan, start praying the Jesus Prayer constantly and with faith. Satan will flee. St. John Climacus says, "With the name of Jesus flog the foes, because there is no stronger weapon in heaven or earth."

Astronauts carry their own atmosphere with them when they enter outer space. In like manner it is possible for the Christian to create his own atmosphere or climate in the soul by the constant use of the Jesus Prayer. So that even though he lives in a sinful world, he will have the power to resist the world of sin which surrounds him.

In science almost every theory is tested in the laboratory. So it is with our Christian faith. It must be tested in the laboratory of life. Try this experiment with your family. Let the last words you utter each night be the Jesus Prayer. Fall asleep with these words on your lips. What better way to end a day than with Jesus? And when you wake up in the morning, let the first words you utter be the Jesus Prayer. What better way to greet a new day than with Jesus? During the day, whether you are talking, sitting, walking, making something, eating or occupied in some way repeat the Jesus Prayer, or the name of Jesus alone in love and adoration. Try this experiment and discover for yourself what countless others have discovered, among them Princess Illeana of Romania. She wrote:

> *Prayer has always been of very real importance to me and the habit formed in early childhood of morning and evening prayer has never left me; but in the practice of the Jesus Prayer I am but a beginner. I would, nonetheless, like to awaken interest in this prayer because, even if I have only touched the hem of a heavenly garment, I have touched it-and the joy is so great I would share it with others . . . .*

She tells how the Jesus Prayer had been helpful to her in surgery. "Jesus," she says, had been her last conscious thought before she went under anesthesia, and the first word on her lips when she came out of surgery. It was marvelous to know, she says, that even during the operation her unconscious mind had been praying the Jesus Prayer: "Lord Jesus, Son of God, have mercy upon me a sinner." For if we fall asleep with the Jesus Prayer, our unconscious mind (which never sleeps) will continue to pray and we will find ourselves waking up with this prayer on our lips. This is what had happened to Princess Illeana during her surgery.

"When I arise in the morning," she continues, "it (the Jesus Prayer) starts me joyfully upon a new day. When I travel by air, land, or sea, it sings within my breast. When I stand upon a platform to face my listeners, it beats encouragement . . . . At the end of a weary day, when I lay me down to rest, I give my heart over to Jesus: '(Lord), into thy hands I commend my spirit.' I sleep, but my heart, as it beats, prays on: 'Jesus.'"

Tell Them About Death

When the death of a friend or relative occurs, parents should use the opportunity to speak to their children about death. Whether children grow up with healthy or morbid attitudes toward death depends on the way their parents face the subject of death. First impressions are important and these are always picked up from parents.

Orthodox Christians must never speak of death without speaking also of Him Who "by His death trampled down death and to those in the tombs gave life everlasting."

A father once tried to explain the difficult question of death to his little boy. In so doing he made this age-old question so simple, so understandable and so comforting that we will share his explanation with you.

"You know, Donnie, God has planned a home for each one of us in heaven. When He has it all ready. He calls us to come to live there with Him. This morning our Heavenly Father called Grandaddy to come to his new home."

"But he's still here. Will we see him go?" the child inquired.

"He's already gone. What you saw lying there asleep on Grandaddy's bed is only his empty body. It's only the house God gave him to live in here on earth. He doesn't need that any more. We'll lay it away carefully in a beautiful box down in the cemetery."

"Do you remember," he continued, "how Grandaddy used to sit here with tears in his eyes when the pain hurt him? It was because he was so very sick. Our Heavenly Father saw the tears. He knew how Grandaddy felt. I think it must have made Him sad, too. God doesn't like to see any of His children unhappy. God knew, too, that Grandaddy's body wasn't a good home for him anymore."

"Won't he miss us, Daddy?"

"I don't believe he'll miss us, Donnie, because in heaven there isn't any kind of sadness. There aren't any tears at all and there is no pain."

The father could no longer hold back the flood of tears. Then came the hardest question of all.

"But Daddy, why are you crying?"

"Because we miss him so!" he sobbed. Then regaining his composure, he said, "We want Grandaddy to be with God and not to be sick or in pain any more, but we will miss him very much."

Your children will have many questions about death as they grow to adulthood. These should always be answered in a straightforward and honest manner.

Children often think that they will never die. Because of this, they ignore the danger of smoking, alcohol, drugs, promiscuous sex, etc. They need to be taught that life is short, that one day they will die and that they will have to answer to God for what they did with the gift of life.

Teaching Our Children About Memorial Prayers for the Dead

Our Orthodox Christian faith takes death frankly and openly into account. Our church calendar provides many occasions when we are asked to face up to the fact of death. Easter is one such occasion. Sunday is another. Every Sunday is a "little Easter" on our church calendar celebrating Christ's victory over death. On our church calendar every year there are special Memorial Saturdays or "Saturdays of the Souls" which provide another opportunity for us to face up to death. On these Saturdays the divine liturgy is celebrated and special prayers are offered for our deceased loved ones. We pray for the dead especially on Saturdays since it was on the Sabbath day that Christ lay dead in the tomb, "resting from all His works" and "trampling down death by death." Thus, in the New Testament, Saturday becomes the proper day for remembering the dead and offering prayers for them.

Why Do We Pray for the Dead?

Christianity is a religion of love. Praying for the dead is an expression of love. We ask God to remember our departed loved ones because we love them. Love relationships survive death and even transcend it. There is an inner need for a relationship with a loved one to continue to be expressed even after a loved one has died. Often *even more so* after a loved one has died since physical communication is no longer possible. The church encourages us to express our love for our departed brethren through memorial services and prayers.

The anniversary of the death of a loved one is very painful. The church helps us cope with this pain by encouraging us to have memorial prayers offered in church for our departed loved ones on the anniversaries of their deaths, i.e., 40 days after the death, six months, a year, etc. This gives us the opportunity to *do* something for our loved one. It helps express and resolve our grief.

Death may take loved ones out of sight but it certainly does not take them out of mind, or out of heart. We continue to love them and think of them as we believe they continue to love and think of us. How can a mother forget a child who has passed over to the life beyond? The same Christian love which led her to pray for that child when he lived will lead her to pray for him now. For in Christ all are living.

A Meaningful Custom

It is customary among Orthodox Christians from Greece to bring a tray of boiled wheat kernels to church for the memorial service. The wheat kernels express belief in everlasting life. Jesus said, "Unless a grain of wheat falls into the earth and dies, it remains alone, but if it dies, it bears much fruit" (John 12:24). Just as new life rises from the buried kernel of wheat, so we believe that the one buried will rise one day to a new life with God. The wheat kernels are covered with sugar and raisins to express the bliss of eternal life with God in heaven.

A Family Project

On the anniversary of the death of a loved one (forty days, six months, one year, two years, etc.), or on the

Memorial Saturdays (consult your Church calendar for dates), make it a project during your "family evening" to make a list of all friends and relatives who have died. Involve the children in the making of the list and assign one of them to give the list personally to your parish priest. Make sure you place a note above the list of names stating, "Father, please pray for our loved ones who have departed to be with the Lord: names . . . ."

If you wish to bring a tray of boiled wheat to church for the memorial prayers, make it a family project. Purchase a pound or two of wheat kernels from a health food store, boil it, place it in a plate, mix raisins in with it, cover it with granulated white sugar, and using raisins or almonds, trace the initials of the deceased person above the sugar together with the sign of the cross. Involve the children in the preparation of the wheat explaining its meaning as you do so (as outlined above). Assign one of the children to carry the plate to the altar before the liturgy and present it to the priest.

Such prayers for the dead benefit also those who pray for the departed. They remind us that we too are going to die; they strengthen faith in the life beyond; they nourish reverence toward those who have died; they help build hope in divine mercy; they develop brotherly love among those who survive. They make us more cautious and diligent in getting ready for that ultimate journey which will unite us with our departed loved ones and usher us into the presence of God. They remind us that now is the time for moral development and improvement: for faith, repentance and love; now is the time to strive for the crown of righteousness which the Lord, the righteous Judge, will award to those "who have fought the good fight, finished the course and kept the faith."

Memorial prayer services, which affirm the reality of

physical death but also the reality of resurrection unto life eternal, play a vital role in teaching our children to cope with grief in a constructive Christian way.

An Old Russian Family Custom

In old Russia a service was held every Easter Sunday afternoon in the village cemetery. Having ended the service in the cemetery chapel, the priest accompanied by acolytes and choir led a procession through the cemetery singing, "Christos Boskres" or "Christ is risen." Stopping at graves where family members stood by in memory of their departed loved ones, the priest greeted each group with this proclamation, "Christ is risen!" and they replied with the same happy assurance, "Truly, He is risen!" What a dramatic expression of our Orthodox Christian faith! To walk through a cemetery on Easter Sunday and sing, "Christ is risen!" Perhaps we can revive this meaningful custom by visiting the graves of loved ones every Easter as a family and singing our glorious Easter hymn "Christ is risen."

Recipe for Preparing Boiled Wheat

5 lb. whole wheat
1 ½ lb. sesame seed
4 cups chopped walnuts
2 ½ cups granulated sugar
4 tsp. cinnamon
½ cup chopped parsley
3 boxes currants
1 box confectioners' sugar-for topping
2 cups flour-for topping

3 oz. silver dragees-for topping
Powdered sugar

Pour wheat in a large canning kettle and cover generously with water. Allow to stand overnight. In the morning, drain and cover with fresh water. Cook about four hours or until tender. Stir often with wooden spoon to keep from sticking. Drain and spread on a large cloth to absorb excess moisture. Bake sesame seed and flour in separate shallow baking pans in a moderate oven, stirring often. Mix other ingredients and mound slightly on a medium sized serving tray. Sprinkle confectioners' sugar and press down with waxed paper to make a smooth compact top. Make a cross on top with silver dragees. On either side of the cross, form the initials of deceased with powdered sugar. This amount is enough for a tray of approximately 50 servings.

Using Incense in the Home

The Orthodox Church brings the good news of Jesus to the total person. She appeals not just to the eye and the ear but also to the sense of smell. A blind and deaf person entering an Orthodox church would recognize immediately that he is in a sacred place through the fragrant smell of the incense.

We read in the book of Revelation, "And I saw an angel come and stand before the altar, having a golden censer; and there was given to him much incense, and the smoke of the incense of the prayers of the saints ascended up before God from the hand of the angel."

The clouds of fragrant smoke emanating from the censer symbolize our prayers ascending to God. The "fragrance" of the incense expresses the delight God takes in our prayers.

The early Christians were required by the pagan Romans to burn a pinch of incense each year publicly before a statue of Caesar. By burning incense before Caesar's statue they would acknowledge that he was divine. Christians refused to perform this act because they considered it idolatrous. For them there was only one Lord-Jesus Christ. For their refusal to burn incense before Caesar they were thrown to the lions.

Today the Orthodox priest burns incense before the holy altar. He censes the Holy Gifts (Communion) and the icons. In other words, we burn incense today before the one true God and none other. The act of burning incense before Jesus confesses our faith that He alone is Lord.

After the priest censes the altar and the icons, he turns and censes the worshippers. By this act he pays homage and respect to the icon of God that abides in us, i.e., the image of God in which we were created. This act reminds us that we are important persons in God's eyes, i.e., His living, walking images.

Every Orthodox home should have a small portable home censer next to the family icon. Parents can teach their children how to light the charcoal and place a piece of incense on it when family prayers are offered. Some parents may prefer to light the censer only on Saturday evenings and on evenings preceding major holy days. The meaning of the incense may be explained to the children from an early age so that they may participate meaningfully in this worshipful act.

A good practice would be for the parents to make the sign of the cross with the censer before each child explaining that by this act they are paying respect to the image of God in them.

Imagine how many beautiful memories this act can instill in children. Every time they come to church as adults they will associate the fragrant incense with a host of endearing memories from their family prayers as children at home. Every time they see the priest censing the altar and the people in the liturgy, they will stand in awe in the presence of the Lord. They will see in the rising smoke their own prayers ascending to the throne of God.

Every week one mother lights a small home censer and takes it to every room in the house asking Christ to bless each room with His presence. The fragrant smoke of the censer fills each room with a holy presence. All week long the children feel (smell) Christ's presence in every room of that house. The same fragrant incense they associate with church is experienced at home. Children come to realize that there is a connection between church and home. The home, too, is sacred. What we do at church, we do also at home. The result is that faith, when it is lived out at home, becomes real.

The Family Icon

A Japanese girl in an American college was invited to spend the Christmas holidays with a classmate. Afterwards she was asked how she enjoyed the holidays. "Very well," she replied, "but I missed God in the home. I have seen you worship God in your church. In my country we have a god-shelf so we can worship our gods in our homes. Do not Americans worship their God in their homes?"

It has been traditional for Orthodox homes to have such a "God-shelf" in the form of an icon with a votive light burning before it. This serves as a reminder of God's presence in the home and as a center for family prayer. In old Russia, for example, every house-from the great winter palace of the Czar to the thatched hut of a peasant-had an icon of Christ or the Virgin Mother. At that time no Russian home was a home until it was consecrated by the icon.

Helen Iswolsky writes in her book *Christ in Russia*,

"In the old days . . . a Russian entering his home or visiting a friend would first of all bow low before the icons and make the sign of the cross before greeting his host. The icons symbolized God's presence; they were a constant reminder of the supernatural life, and appealed to morality and conscience. It is difficult to lie, to cheat, or to be brutal in front of an icon.

In fact, if the Church in Russia did survive under Communism, despite lack of any facilities for instructing children in the Christian faith either at school or at church, it is due (humanly speaking) to the Christian family. Throughout Orthodox Christendom the family has been regarded as a "house church" with its own "altar" where prayers are offered before the icons.

The icon is more than a "visual aid" for the Orthodox Christian. It is in effect a sacrament. For, an icon is not fully an icon until it has been blessed. Then it becomes a link between the human and the divine. It provides an existential encounter between man and God. It becomes the place of an appearance of Christ, provided one stands before it with the right disposition of heart and mind. It becomes a place of prayer. An icon participates in the event it depicts and is almost a re-creation of that event existentially for the believer. As Fr. Bulgakov said, "By the blessing of the icon of Christ, a mystical meeting of the faithful and Christ is made possible."

If you do not have an icon in your home, ask your priest where you can purchase one. If possible, involve the entire family in the selection and purchase of the family icon. Once purchased, take it to church as a family for the blessing. If desired, you may involve the members of the family in the decision as to where the family icon will be placed in the home. In addition to the one official family icon, children may have icons of their own in their rooms. In each case the icon should be first blessed by the priest.

After having spend much time in Russia in the late 19th century, Stephen Graham wrote the following about the importance of the icon in the Russian home,

Every Russian home has its Icons . . . The Icon claims the home and the man for God; it indicates God's ownership . . . It (the Icon) is in religion what the trademark is in commerce . . . In every Russian room there is an Icon, even in railway waiting rooms, public houses, prison cells . . . It occupies what is known as the front corner of every room, that is, the *corner towards the rising sun; it is not strictly proper to sit with one's back to it, and indeed peasants' tables are often arranged so that it is impossible to sit with one's back to it . . . If you sleep in a Russian home, the Icon with its little lamp before it, looks down upon you all night . . . In reverence to the Icon you remove your hat upon entering a room-it is a sign that God is in the room with you . . . It owns the room, or rather is a Presence in the room . . . Outside are the sun and moon and stars . . . inside, the Icon takes their place.**

* *Undiscovered Russia*, Stephen Graham. Bodley Head Press. London. 1912

How to Make a Family Prayer Corner

Here are a few suggestions on how to establish a prayer corner in your home.

- Clear the floor and wall area in a corner or along one wall of a room, preferably facing east, the source of the true light, God who "has called us out of dark ness into his marvelous light" (1 Peter 2:4).
- Lay a piece of carpet to make kneeling or sitting easier, and provide a few cushions, and a prayer stool or firm chair.
- Select a small, low table so that it is accessible from a kneeling position.
- The table may be covered with a white linen cloth.
- On the table place a Bible open to the reading of the day, a candle or votive lamp and a small jar or vase of flowers. The lamp may be lit before dawn and at nightfall as part of our "spiritual worship" (Rom. 12:1).
- A small cross or crucifix may be placed or hung in the center of the table with an icon of Christ (to the right) and the Mother of God (to the left).
- The table may include a drawer or cupboard to store supplies (extra candles, matches, incense, etc.), and a shelf for liturgical and devotional books.

In selecting a cross one should find one that depicts not only the suffering and death of Christ but also His victory over death. Other books that may be kept in the domestic prayer corner include the Psalter, other prayer books, and perhaps a prayer rope. Family prayer should be in harmony as much as possible with the church's liturgical year, appropriating the particular prayers, readings, etc. A set of paper icons can be used to highlight the various holy days of the year.* A small family censer may be kept on the table. Children may be assigned the task of lighting the candle, the censer and replenishing the flowers. The prayer corner preserves the "memory of God" in the home and helps us realize that holiness is homemade. In a home with a prayer corner, children grow up "tasting" and experiencing God. Regular family prayer can help turn the home into what someone called "a workshop for growth towards theosis (union with God)." Perhaps we need this even more today when families are so scattered and disconnected. Many Orthodox Christians carry the lighted Paschal candle home with them following the Paschal liturgy to light the *kandili* (votive light) before the family icon with the Paschal flame of the Resurrected Jesus, thus establishing a direct connection between the church and the home.

---

* Icon Packet: Come Bless the Lord is recommended. It contains 40 icons in color, covering the major holy days of the Orthodox Church. 8 1/2" x 11". These may be used according to the festal seasons. Available through Light and Life Publishing Company, Minneapolis, MN.

Keep the Baptismal Candle

The candles used at the baptism of a child in the Orthodox Church are very significant and meaningful. "Today we have escaped from darkness, and by the light of the knowledge of God we have been illuminated," says the prayer of Patriarch Sophronius. Once asleep to the wonders of salvation, baptism opened the eyes of the soul to see Christ, "the true light that enlightens every person coming into the world" (John 1:9).

The baptismal candle should be kept by the parents and presented to the child upon reaching the age of understanding. At this time the parents can explain that at baptism the child received the light of Christ. "I am the light of the world. He who follows Me shall not walk in darkness but shall have the light of life."

His light illumines our steps as we walk through life. It shows us who we are, i.e., children of God, loved by Him, cared for by Him, created and redeemed by Him. It reminds us that He will walk with us through life to illumine our path. It shows us the way to union with Him both now and for all eternity. Jesus is the real light and the only light for the Christian, revealing to us our identity and our destiny.

In the early Church the baptismal candle was always kept by the person baptized. It was lit every year on the anniversary of the person's baptism and on major holy days. It was brought to church for the Epiphany liturgy every year when one made a renewal of the baptismal vows to renounce the devil and follow Christ. (Epiphany was the day on which most baptisms took place in the early Church.) If the person was married, it was the baptismal candle that was used at the wedding in place of any other candle. If he was ordained, it was used at his ordination. Finally, as death approached, the baptismal candle was again illuminated to express the Christian's faith that death leads not to the darkness of the tomb but to the indescribable brightness of the Transfigured Christ.

Orthodox Christian parents should revive this ancient custom of preserving the baptismal candle of each child, using it as a constant reminder that we are children of the light and encouraging each child to live daily by the light of Christ. The entire family, for example, can attend the liturgy on Epiphany, or the Sunday following Epiphany, to make an annual renewal of their baptismal vows. Each child should be encouraged to use the candle for every major step he takes in life, i.e., marriage, ordination, etc. And, of course, as the child is growing, it can be used every year on the anniversary of the child's baptism when a special party can be held, the details of which are explained in a special chapter of this book.

Tell Them About Confession

A traveler, recently returned from a trip around the world, related how he saw in Japan a man stagger through a railway station with a huge carton on his back. On the carton were the words, "The Universe." An individual bent under the weight of the universe! How graphically this describes what has happened to the individual. Through books, newspapers, radio and television, the "universe" and its troubles are daily laid on the backs of staggering individuals-individuals who are already loaded with excess baggage of their own.

We shall not deal with the world's problems. We shall concern ourselves rather with our own. For many of us are staggering under the weight of the excess baggage of our hatreds and jealousies, of our fears and worries, of our failures and our secret sins. How can a man carry all this baggage on his shoulders, day after day, month after month, year after year, without breaking under the burden?

God has provided a way for man to rid himself of this excess baggage of sin and guilt. The way is through repentance and confession.

The noted Christian psychiatrist, Dr. Paul Tournier, wrote,

"I have at times been accused of over-emphasizing the importance of confession, as if the whole cure of souls were contained in it. I speak from my own experience as a doctor . . . (nothing) can be compared in importance with confession.

"I could give very many examples, especially of patients who have come to visit me only once often from a great distance with the sole purpose of finding someone to whom they could confess a sin that has been weighing upon them for years . . . . There remained nothing for me to do but to remind them in one way or another that if we confess our sins, He (God) is faithful and just, to forgive us our sins and to cleanse us from all unrighteousness (1 John 1:9) . . . . There is no worse suffering than a guilty conscience, and certainly none more harmful . . . . The tremendous joy brought by forgiveness plays an important part in causing the medical effects (of healing) to which I have referred. In many cases I have seen a physical illness disappear overnight after the confession of a lie or an illicit love-affair."*

This is not a clergyman speaking. This is a psychiatrist. And he speaks from his own clinical experience.

Blessed are Those Who Mourn

"Blessed are those who mourn," said Jesus, "for they shall be comforted." Mourn for what? Mourn for their sins. Among all those who mourn, none-says Jesus-shall be sooner consoled than those who weep for their own sins. Sin is the only evil that can be cured by mourning.

Is Any Sin Unforgivable?

A distressed mother came to her priest one day with the excited confession, "Father, I have committed the unpardonable sin!"

The priest showed no sign of surprise but simply asked her in a restrained and quiet voice: "Are you sorry for it?"

"Yes, Father, dreadfully sorry!" was her anguished reply.

---

* *The Doctor's Casebook*, Dr. Paul Tournier. Harper and Row. 1960.

"Then you have committed nothing that cannot be forgiven. There is no sin, no matter how great, that cannot be forgiven by Jesus when a person is truly sorrowful."

Sorrow in the Heart

Before we confess with the tongue, there must always be sorrow in the heart, sorrow that we have disobeyed a loving God. This sorrow of the heart we call repentance. Unless there is sorrow and repentance in the heart, no sin can be forgiven no matter how many times we come to the sacrament of confession. The mouth must always confess out of an abundance of sorrow in the heart.

Why Confession?

But why the Sacrament of Confession? you ask. Can't I confess directly to God? Why confess to a priest who is subject to human weakness like myself? Why confess to a man?

The truth of the matter is that the church urges us to confess our sins directly to God *every day in our prayers*. Confession of sin is a part of every true prayer. But in addition to this, God has given us the Sacrament of Confession. It was He Who gave His apostles the power to forgive sin in His name. His words to them were:

"As the Father has sent Me, I also send you. Receive the Holy Spirit, whose sins you shall forgive, they are forgiven them; whose sins you shall retain, they are retained" (John 20:20-23).

The priest is merely an instrument in confession-as he is an instrument in Baptism and Communion-an instrument through which Christ our Lord pronounces His forgiveness to the penitent sinner. Forgiveness does not emanate from the priest; it emanates from Christ. That is why the priest does not say, "I forgive you . . . ." but "May our Lord Jesus forgive you . . . ."

God chose priests not angels, said St. Chrysostom. He chose weak beings to forgive other weak beings because they would *understand.*

When a person sins, he separates himself not only from God but also from the family of God-the church. By confessing to another man-the priest-the sinner is united not only to God but also to the people of God-the church *He is accepted and* made to feel that he is once more part of the family of God.

There is no sin that God will not forgive. He forgave David who had committed murder and adultery. If He forgave David and surrounded his life with grace once more, surely He will forgive us. "Though your sins be as scarlet, they shall be as white as snow" (Isaiah 1:18).

The only person who cannot be forgiven is the one who thinks he has no sin and does not come to God for forgiveness. And it seems that this is the case with quite a number of people today. "Why should I come to confession?" they say. "I haven't killed anyone. I haven't stolen. If anyone should come to confession, it's so-and-so who hurt me and did me such a great injustice."

Who can say he is without sin when the Word of God says, "If we say we have no sin, we deceive ourselves, and the truth is not in us" (1 John 1:8). Who can say he is without sin when Jesus says, "If any one would sue you and take your coat, let him have your cloak as well; and if any one forces you to go one mile, go with him two miles" (Matthew 5:40-41)? Have we kept these commandments? Who can say he is without sin? Only he who has not examined his life. Only he whom the devil has deceived, for Satan delights in hiding our sins and pointing out to us only the sins of others.

Daily Confession

Since we sin daily, we should confess daily. Confession is not something that is to be put off for a few rare occasions during the year. We must repent and confess our sins to Jesus daily in prayer if we are to receive His forgiveness daily. Why is it that Jesus taught us to pray in the model prayer, "Forgive us our trespasses"? Isn't it because He wants us to come to Him daily in prayer for forgiveness? Repentance and confession were never meant to be limited exclusively to the Sacrament of Confession. The repentance and confession that should precede Holy Communion should be a *daily* repentance and a *daily* confession. Daily confession is essential to a healthy and growing spiritual life in Christ.

Augustine said once, "Baptism is for all sins. For light sins without which we cannot be, there is prayer. What prayer? 'Forgive us our trespasses!' Only once we are washed in baptism; *but daily are we washed by prayer.*" Augustine tells us elsewhere that the Sacrament of Confession is mandatory for grave sins.

Speaking of repentance, St. Chrysostom writes, "Behold, we have pointed five ways of repentance. First, the acknowledgment of our sins; secondly, forgiving the sins of our neighbor; thirdly, through prayer; fourthly, through almsgiving; fifthly, humility. Do not delay, but take all of these ways each day." These five essentials of repentance should be emphasized to our children.

Thus, in addition to the Sacrament of Confession for-

giveness of sins is granted through:
1) Prayer ("Forgive us our trespasses")
2) Holy Communion ("The servant of God - - - receives the Precious Body and Blood of Christ *for the for giveness of sins* and unto life everlasting").
3) Holy Unction (James 4:13-15)
4) The prayers of forgiveness found in the liturgy and the other services of the Church.

Orthodox Christian parents can create an atmosphere at home where prayers for forgiveness are offered daily. During family prayer time, children may be encouraged to confess their sins by using the following ritual: Child: "For (sin)…" The group responds: "Forgive us, O Lord."

Consult your parish priest as to how often your family should come to the Sacrament of Confession.

To confess our sins to God is not to tell Him anything He doesn't already know. But until we confess them, they remain a wall separating us from Him. Once we confess them, they become a bridge leading to God's forgiveness and acceptance.

Staretz Silouan said once, "The slave justifies (excuses) himself, but the son admits his guilt." We are God's sons and daughters-not slaves.

A Father Who Understands

Little Jimmy had just spilled some paint on the back porch. He had tried not to, but he *did*!

"What will your father say?" asked his frightened playmate. "Aw, he'll understand," was Jimmy's confident reply. And little Jimmy was right. His father did "understand" and willingly forgave him.

What peace, what joy, and what confidence-to know that in heaven we have such a Father, a Father Who understands, Who knows us personally by our very names, and Who, knowing us, forgives us.

Forgiveness is a costly thing for Jesus. He paid very dearly for it on the cross. But for us He has made forgiveness easy. He could have asked much more of us in the way of atonement. But He asks only that we lay bare our wounds that He may pour over them the healing drops of His precious blood.

Man's life is indeed burdened with excess baggage, the heaviest of which is guilt. The answer to the needs of man in this matter is not a vacation, a sleeping pill or a trip to the psychiatrist. Christ gives the answer in His gift to us of repentance and confession. Here we may unburden our soul of the guilt that dogs our steps and racks our mind when we have offended God. It is Christ's answer to the sins of His children. It brings to the heart "the peace of God that surpasses all human understanding."

One of the reasons some young people seldom attend the Sacrament of Confession is that they rarely see their parents go to confession. After talking to their children about this sacrament, parents should make it a point to attend the sacrament with their children. The example of the parents is crucial.

Forgiveness Prayer

My failure to be true even to my own accepted standards:
My self-deception in the face of temptation:
My choosing of the worse when I know the better:
O Lord, forgive.

My failure to apply to myself the standards of
conduct I demand of others:
My blindness to the suffering of others, and my
slowness to be taught by my own:
My complacence towards wrongs that do not touch
my own case and my over-sensitiveness to
those that do:
My slowness to see the good in my fellows and
to see the evil in myself:
My hardness of heart towards my neighbor's
faults, and my readiness to make allowance for my own:
O Lord, forgive.

For Further Reading

If We Confess Our Sins by T. Hopko. A pamphlet (78 pages)
that helps one prepare for confession. Includes prayers before and
after confession.

We Return to God. Preparing children for confession.
Pamphlet.

These are the Sacraments. Anthony M. Coniaris.

Making Things Right: The Sacrament of Reconciliation J.T.
Leichner. OCEC.

*Nicholas Wins the Prize: Young Nicholas Experiences the
Sacrament of Confession* by Helen Iakovos-Dalalakis. For ele-
mentary ages. Light and Life Publ. Co.

Bake A Loaf of Altar Bread and Bring it to Church

A very meaningful project for the Orthodox Christian family is to bake a loaf of altar bread and bring it to church for the liturgy.

The significance of the bread may be explained as follows.

Jesus said, "I am the living bread which came down from heaven; if any one eat of this bread, he will live forever; and the bread which I shall give for the life of the world is my flesh" (John 6:51).

St. Paul writes, "The Lord Jesus on the night when he was betrayed took bread, and when he had given thanks, he broke it and said, 'This is my body which is broken for you. Do this in remembrance of me'" (I Cor. 11:23).

Jesus is the bread of life Who offers Himself for our salvation. "Unless you eat the flesh of the Son of man and drink his blood you have no life in you; he who eats my flesh and drinks my blood has eternal life, and I will raise him up at the last day" (John 6:53-54).

The altar bread represents Jesus Who is the Bread of life. It is baked by someone in the congregation and brought to the priest for each liturgy. You may contact your priest to let him know that your family would like to bake a loaf of altar bread for a certain liturgy. In many Slavic churches five small loaves are used to commemorate the five loaves which Jesus blessed and multiplied.

The Gift of Ourselves

Bread is used not only to represent Jesus Who is the Bread of life, of which if any man eat he shall never hunger, but also to express the offering of our life to God. The Greek word for altar bread is *prosphora* which means an *offering* to God. Bread is used as an offering because it represents life. It is the staff of life. Once consumed it becomes part of us, i.e., flesh and bones. Thus, in presenting the loaf of bread to God, we are, in effect, offering our life to Him. It is the gift of our love.

The priest accepts the gift and places it on the holy altar. This act represents God accepting our gift. It now passes into His possession. God is so pleased with the gift of our life that He transforms it through the Holy Spirit and gives it back to us as His Precious Body. Thus it is that communion with God results. We give ourselves to God and He, in turn, gives Himself to us.

Stamped with a Seal

A special seal is stamped on top of the loaf before it is baked. Your priest will know where you can borrow or purchase such a seal. The middle part of the seal contains a square piece of bread with the words IC and XC. This is a Greek abbreviation for JESUS CHRIST. Since this is the piece that will be changed into the Body of Christ, it is called the *Lamb of God*. A large triangular piece is removed from the left of the Lamb of God and placed on the paten. This represents the Virgin Mary, our Lord's mother. Then nine smaller triangular pieces are removed from the seal to commemorate the angels, prophets, apostles and saints of the church. These are placed on the paten to the right of the Lamb of God. Following this, the priest prays for the living members of the congregation especially for those whose names have been submitted. As he prays for each name, he cuts a small piece of bread, representing the person prayed for, and places it immediately below Jesus, the Lamb of God. Finally, he removes a piece of bread for each deceased person for whom we have requested prayers. Thus, around the Lamb of God on the paten is gathered the entire church consisting of the angels, saints, and loved ones in heaven together with members of the local congregation. ALL are living in God's presence and all constitute the one living Body of Christ.

Since the loaf represents us, it is recommended that the family submit a list of names to the priest together with the loaf. One column should be entitled LIVING, listing the names of members of the immediate family who have baked the bread plus any others they wish to have remembered in prayer. A second column should be entitled DEPARTED under which may be listed the names of loved ones now with God in heaven.

A Prayer

After the bread has been baked, the following prayer may be said in unison by the family:

Dear Lord, this bread that we have baked represents each one of us in this family and in our congregation. We are offering ourselves to You, our very life, in humble obedience and total commitment to You. We place ourselves on Your holy altar through this bread

*to be used by You in any way that You feel will help
enlarge Your kingdom. Accept our gift and make us
worthy to receive the greater gift that You will give us
when You consecrate this bread and give it back to us
as Your Precious Body. Amen.*

We Are on the Altar

By baking the altar bread and bringing it to church, we
come to realize that we are not only *at* the altar but *on* the
altar in every liturgy. The bread and wine which the priest
places on the altar represent us. When the priest elevates the
bread and wine (chalice and paten) at the altar, we kneel. We
remember that these are our gifts the priest is offering to
God: our love, our thanksgiving, our obedience, our life. We
remember that we are *on* the altar offering ourselves to God.

Once the bread is baked it may be taken to the church and
presented to the priest by the entire family. This act involves
everyone in the offering of the gift. Each family may decide
how often they would like to prepare the altar bread in con-
sultation with the priest.

Altar Bread (Prosphora) Recipe

For one large loaf or five small loaves use:
   3 ½ cups high-gluten flour, sifted ("All Purpose"
   flour is modestly high in gluten.)
   1 teaspoon of dry yeast
   a dash of salt
   1 cup luke warm water

1. Dissolve the yeast in warm water and set aside.
2. Combine the flour and salt in a large bowl. Form a well in the flour.
3. Add the dissolved yeast to the flour mixture.
4. Mix well, adding a bit more flour if the dough is sticky, up to 1 cup.
5. Sprinkle a little flour on a board or table/counter top and begin kneading the dough until it becomes smooth and stiff.
6. Place the dough in a bowl, cover, and let rise one-half hour in a warm place.
7. Form the dough into a ball, flatten with the palm of your hand, and roll it gently with a rolling pin.
8. Place it in a 9" floured baking pan.
9. Dip the prosphora seal in flour, and then tap off the excess.
10. Firmly press the seal in the center of the dough. Keep the pressure on the seal for as long as it takes to pray the Lord's Prayer, then remove the seal very carefully.
11. Cover the pan with a clean lint-free towel and let rise in a warm place about one hour until the bread doubles in size.
12. Preheat the oven to 350 degrees.

13. Bake for approximately 30 minutes.
14. Remove the bread from the pan and set it on a cooling rack.
15. Allow the *prosphora* to cool completely before wrapping in plastic or aluminum foil for transport to church.

To make five small loaves (Slavic tradition), replace the above steps 7 through 10 with:

- Roll out the dough to a level ¾-inch thickness on a well-floured board, and cut out five rounds with a 3-inch biscuit cutter or the drinking end of a glass. Transfer rounds to a floured cookie sheet.
- Re-roll the remaining dough to a level ½-inch thickness and cut out five 2 ½-inch rounds with a cutter/glass. Press the *prosphora* seal on the top of each small round and remove carefully.
- Dampen the tops of the 3-inch rounds with water, and prick several times with a straight pin; use a spatula to place one of the smaller rounds centered, on top of each of the larger rounds; press lightly to "seal" the rounds together.

How to Explain the Liturgy to Your Children

I once heard someone day how dinner was served down on the farm in the old days. All the children and the hired help come in from the fields at noon. They wash their hands and sit at the table. Before the food is served, the mail is read. Then the instructions are given as to which chores must be completed that afternoon and evening. After this is finished, the food is served to give everyone the strength to carry out the instructions just received.

Something similar takes place in every liturgy. In the first part of the liturgy-called the Liturgy of the Word-we receive the Word of God. God gives us his instructions as to what He wants us to do, how He wants us to live. We receive these instructions in the Epistle lesson, the Gospel lesson, and the sermon. But we are too weak to carry out the Word of God. We lack strength. That is why in the second part of the liturgy-called the Liturgy of the Faithful-God gives us the power we need. He gives us Himself-the Bread of Life-through the Sacrament of Holy Communion.

What is Holy Communion? How can we best prepare for it?

Dr. Panayiotis Trembelas, professor of theology at the University of Athens, wrote that when Christ was born in Bethlehem of Judea, He chose to be born not of a mother who was listed in "Who's Who," but of a poor, humble, pure peasant girl. He chose as His place of entry into this world not a palace but a cold, damp cave that served as a stable for animals. Who would have thought at the time that this child born of this humble mother in such a desolate place was God himself? Yet doesn't this very same thing happen again in the

Sacrament of Holy Communion? Doesn't the all-powerful Christ, Lord of heaven and earth, who holds the whole world in His hands, who is worshipped by all creation, doesn't He, even in this sacrament, shed His divine glory and majesty to come to us under the humble forms of bread and wine?

What happened in Bethlehem long ago happens again today whenever the liturgy is celebrated. Christ comes to us again quietly, humbly, disguised under the forms of bread and wine. Have you ever imagined what would happen if Christ were to descend on the altar with the same glorified body with which the disciples saw Him ascending into heaven? Who of us would dare approach Him? Or if He should offer us His body as it was when it was taken down from the cross on Good Friday? Who of us would dare touch it? Through the great Sacrament of Holy Communion the Lord makes himself utterly approachable, disguising himself, even as He did in the manger, and coming to us ever so humbly under the forms of bread and wine. The Sacrament of Communion is the perpetuation of Christmas. In celebrating Christmas we observe not only God's coming into the world thousands of years ago; we celebrate also His coming into the world today to be born in the manger of our soul though this great sacrament in every liturgy.

A faithful Orthodox family should receive Christ in the Eucharist as often as possible. The Lord Jesus invites us to receive Him in every liturgy. His personal invitation to us is, "Take, eat, this is my body . . . Drink ye all of it, this is my blood. . . ."

Parents are encouraged to share the above facts with their children before coming to the Sacrament.

For Further Reading

For the Life of the World by A. Schmemann.
Living the Liturgy by S. Harakas. Excellent and practical.
The Divine Liturgy for Children-An Interactive Guide for Participation in the Divine Liturgy. This is most helpful for parents to use with children.

Living Out the Fullness of the Liturgical Life in the Home

In our Orthodox tradition, the child begins to experience from early childhood the fullness of liturgical life. He kisses the cross; he tastes the holy Eucharist; he lights the candles; he kisses the icons; he says the magic words of the Lord's Prayer. These are excellent practices. The child is beginning to "catch" the faith. But all of these practices have no connection with the outside world of football, cars, school, etc. To the child, the real things have some connection with everyday life. If they have no connection to everyday life, they are not as real. But when that same child sees the icons that he sees at church at home, and smells the same fragrant incense that he smells at church at home, and hears the priest reading the same Gospel lesson in church that his parents read to him at home, and sees the parents who pray at church praying at home, then something critical happens. Faith, brought home and practiced at home, becomes real! So let the child *kiss* the cross, *taste* the holy Eucharist, *kiss* the icons, *light* the candle and *say* the magic words of prayer before bed and meals-*only let him say them with mom and dad both at home and at church.*

The Kissingest Church

Kissing is a common part of worship in the Orthodox Church. Most Protestants and Roman Catholics don't kiss as much as we Orthodox do in our worship services. We kiss icons, crosses, Gospel books. We kiss the edge of the priest's robe, his hand, the chalice. I'm sure we would kiss even the censer if we didn't fear we would get burned! St. John

Chrysostom makes the charming assertion that because we receive the Holy Eucharist through our lips, our lips are most blessed, and we honor them by giving kisses.

When Are We in Condition to Receive Holy Communion?

Fulton Oursler tells about an incident in his childhood when his mother, after dressing him in his Sunday best, warned him not to get off the front steps. "We'll be walking over to see your aunt," she promised, "and I want you to be neat."

He waited obediently until the baker's son came along and called him a sissy. Soon they got into a fight and the next thing Fulton knew he was sitting in the middle of a mud puddle. With a twinge of conscience he returned to the front steps.

Presently, down the street came the ice-cream peddler, pushing his cart. Forgetting his disobedience, Fulton ran indoors and begged his mother for a penny.

"Just look at yourself!" she exclaimed. "You're in no condition to ask for anything."

There are many persons who feel the same way about receiving Communion. How often we hear people say, "I'm in no condition to receive Communion." When is a person "in condition" to receive Communion?

Have you ever had the feeling on a particular occasion that you shouldn't take Communion? Many of us have that feeling occasionally. We feel unworthy; we feel that it would by hypocritical to take Communion; we feel that we aren't "good enough" to participate. I think this is a good feeling to have before Communion. No Christian should ever come to Communion with the feeling that he deserves to come because he is "good enough." If anyone has this feeling, he should not come. For this is a good sign that he is not good enough; that his soul has been poisoned by the sin of pride.

There is one thing we should always remember about Communion. And it is this: When the Lord Jesus invites us to Communion, He is calling us not to PERFECTION but to CONFESSION. If we are not "good enough"-as none of us is-then let us repent and come to confession to receive the Lord's forgiveness, to let Him cleanse us, to let Him make us worthy. "Him that cometh to me I will in no way cast out," said Jesus.

It is important to let our children know when they are in condition to receive Christ. We must keep the door open for them to keep coming to this great sacrament which unites us to Christ and to each other.

How Holy Communion Makes Us One Body In Christ

Most of us are aware of the vertical dimension of the Eucharist, of the fact that it unites us to God as His people: "He who eats my flesh and drinks my blood abides in me and I in him," said Jesus. It is this sacrament which makes it possible for us to say with St. Paul, "Christ lives in me." And through this sacrament, we can leave the Lord's table with the glowing courage of the same St. Paul who said, "I can do all things through Christ who strengthens me."

Few Christians, however, realize the horizontal dimension of the Eucharist, the fact that it unites us not only to God, but also to each other. Through the Eucharist we all become one in Christ since the same Christ dwells in all of us. The Fathers of the Church take for granted the unity of the individual to God through the Eucharist. What they stress and emphasize greatly is the horizontal dimension of Communion-our becoming one with each other in Christ. "The very fact that we all share one bread makes us one body," says St. Paul.

Christ tells us that the first and greatest commandment is love of God and man. Yet we all know from experience that it is not always easy to love our fellow man. God knew that this was a difficult commandment. That is why He gave us the Sacrament of Communion through which He gives us His own strength to enable us to practice this commandment of love.

The Orthodox Church emphasizes love. Dr. Otto Nall, former Bishop of the Methodist Church in Minnesota, wrote, "Orthodoxy stresses love . . . if Roman Catholic Christianity is the religion of the 'law,' and Protestant Christianity is the religion of 'faith,' then Orthodox Christianity is the religion of 'love'. That shines through all of its life."

If Orthodox Christianity is the religion of love, it is so because it believes not only that we are all created in the image of God, and that Christ died for all and that all are called to the resurrection in the new life, but Orthodoxy is the religion of love especially because it believes that through the Eucharist Christ comes to live in us, making us all a community of brothers and sisters. This is why the liturgy is never celebrated in private, just by the priest alone, but always with the family of God-the congregation-present. This is done in order to express the horizontal dimension of the Eucharist, i.e., the fact that by receiving the Body and Blood of Christ we are all joined together in one body, one family-the family of God.

This means that the same Christ who comes to us in Holy Communion comes to us also in the person of our neighbor, our fellow parishioner, our fellow Christian: Christ lives in every person I meet. "Forasmuch as you did it unto one of these the least of my brethren you did it to me," said Jesus. The way I treat my fellow man is the way I treat Christ. To honor Christ in the Sacrament of Communion and dishonor Him in the person of my neighbor is sacrilege, sin, hypocrisy. St. John Chrysostom writes, "Do you wish to honor the Body of Christ? Then do not look down or disdain Him when you see Him in rags. After having honored Him in church with silken vestments do not leave Him to die of cold outside for lack of clothing. For it is the same Jesus who says 'This is my Body' and who says 'You saw me hungry and did not give me to eat. What you have refused to the least of these my little ones, you have refused to me!"

The same Christ, then, who comes to us in the Eucharist

comes to us also in the people we meet and with whom we live. The Lord Jesus tells us specifically that we are not to approach the altar to receive His body unless we have first established a relationship of love and forgiveness with all our fellow humans on the horizontal level. "If you are offering your gift at the altar, and there remember that your brother has something against you, leave your gift there before the altar and go: first be reconciled to your brother, and then come and offer your gift" (Matt. 5:23, 24)

Two ideas to consider as a result of what we learned above: (1) decide on a person in need that your family can help in some way; (2) make it a family practice to ask forgiveness from one another at home before receiving Holy Communion.

The Importance of the Parents' Attitude Towards Church and Sunday School

The parents' attitude towards church and Sunday school is crucial. There are parents who are habitually late for church. The result is that the children miss part or most of the liturgy and the Sunday school lesson. The continuity of the lesson is destroyed. The class is continually interrupted by late-comers. The teacher becomes frustrated. But even more important is what happens to the student. The child knows that for important things one has to be on time, i.e., public school for example. The habit of coming to church and Sunday school late teaches the child that God is not as important as public school or the piano lesson for which one has to be on time.

Another example is the attitude of the parents toward coming to church on Sunday. It doesn't take much for some parents to stay away from church: just a little bit of rain will do it. But parents never stay away from work on Monday morning because of rain. So the child's mind learns that work is more important than God. For that matter, almost anything is more important than God. Is it a wonder, then, that children grow up to adopt a system of values that leaves God out entirely?

Punctuality and faithful attendance at church impress upon children the importance of God and of our Orthodox Christian value system.

Get Some Feedback

Parents can evaluate and improve the complex but rewarding role of parentthood by getting some feedback periodically from their children. Here is one way it can be done.

At one of the "family evening sessions" distribute paper and pencil to each child. Have them write a short description of mom and dad as they see each of them. Encourage them to be totally honest.

Parents can receive a pretty good idea as to how they are coming across to their children through such sessions. Proper changes can be made in the life-style of parents as a result of such regular communication. It may surprise some of see how perceptive children can be in evaluating their parents and pointing out inconsistencies of which the parents may be unaware.

It is best to become aware of our shortcomings and to do something about them before they cause lasting harm. It is a tragedy to have a child grow up and tell you years later of some defect in your behavior that caused him to rebel.

We are not saying anything about feedback from the parents to the children. We are assuming that this is going on constantly. It is the children-to-parents feedback that is seldom encouraged.

One important quality of the parent-to-child feedback is that we heed the advice of St. Paul to "Speak the truth in love." It was said of a former teacher and principal that if he ever had occasion to rebuke his students, he did it always with his arm around them. If our warnings are given, not in anger, not in irritation, not in criticism, not in condemnation, not in the desire to hurt, but in love, they will be effective.

Baron von Hugel explained once the rule he followed in

criticizing and reviewing books. He said he always tried to begin his criticism by saying what he could in praise of the book, then he voiced his doubts and objections, and finally in closing the review, he returned again to the book's good points. He was anxious always to wrap the truth in love.

How to Read the Bible at Home

"If I had to form a man from childhood as I thought best, I should like to have him choose a few good passages of Scripture and to make him read them often until he knew them by heart."-*Bossuet*.

During World War II a South Sea islander showed an American GI his copy of the Bible and said, "This is my most prized possession."

With a hint of disdain, the soldier replied, "We've outgrown all that sort of thing, you know."

"It's a good thing we haven't," the islander shot back. "If it wasn't for this Bible, you would have been a meal as soon as we laid eyes on you."

One of the tragedies of many people today is the feeling that they have outgrown the need for God's word. The disaster they bring upon themselves as a result is tragic. But the person who reads the Bible believing that God is actually speaking to him through what he reads-this person's life is transformed. He finds healing, wholeness, power, peace, forgiveness, love and purpose.

A Few Case Histories

Let us examine a few case histories of how this has actually happened in the lives of people.

Most of us remember how Paul's life changed completely after he heard the word of God on the road to Damascus. Some of us recall that the conversion of Augustine the great sinner to Augustine the great saint and bishop happened when he picked up the Bible one day and read a passage that spoke to his soul. But these are old examples. They happened long ago. They do not seem as real as what happens today. So let us take a look at how the Bible has helped people in our day.

Example No. 1. Some years ago we had a famous biochemist from the University of Minnesota, Dr. Fred Smith, address one of our District G.O.Y.A. Conferences in Minneapolis. He delivered one of the most inspiring talks I have ever heard. All of us who were present felt the presence of God that evening. What I did not know at that time was that Dr. Smith had previously been an agnostic. He had rejected the Christianity of his youth. What brought him back to Christ was a Bible verse he heard one day that he simply could not get out of his mind. It was this Bible verse that brought him back to Christ-this time as a truly committed Christian. He became one of the most convincing supporters of Christianity on the University campus. Until his death a few years ago he held a weekly Bible class in his home. From agnostic to Christian because of a Bible verse!

Example No. 2. A certain lady was facing a serious operation. She was frightened even though she knew she had the best doctors and many friends praying for her. Her pastor did his best to comfort her but she was still too frightened for the operation. Then, lying alone in bed one night in the hospital, she opened the Bible and read the Psalms-all of them. A few days later, following surgery, she said to her pastor, "You know, I read all the Psalms the night before my operation. I don't remember a word I read, but I received the strong conviction that God was real and was with me, and my fear vanished."

Example No. 3. A young socialite married to a rich contractor felt a deep emptiness in her life. Nothing pleased her. She took to drinking. Her marriage was on the verge of divorce. Musing one day that psychiatrists had been of no help, she impulsively purchased a Bible and began reading it. After reading right through the night, she suddenly felt what she later described as "the most marvelous feeling of peace and release." Her emptiness was filled by God. She and her husband became changed persons-saved from alcoholism and divorce by the word of God.

Why Its Enduring Power?

Why is it that this Book has had such enduring power through the centuries? The only answer is that it is God's Book. It speaks, as no other book can, to the heart and needs of man. It answers questions basic to life: Who am I? Why am I here? Where am I going? It speaks with power. The word of God contained in the Bible is not merely an "inspiring thought" or a "good idea"; it is a power which transforms the lives of those who accept it; it is the "power of God unto salvation to everyone who believes," writes St. Paul.

Moreover, the Bible speaks with ultimate authority. Nothing has so shaken our security these days as the philosophy of relativism, the so-called "New Morality"-the theory that holds ultimate truth to be a mirage; the theory that no values are fixed, that each person decides existentially in each situation what is right and what is wrong. Against this spineless fluidity the Bible says, "Thus saith the Lord." God has spoken. He has given us goalposts. He has given us stars to steer by. He has given us principles that are valid not for a few generations but forever. As someone so well said, "God gave us commandments; He did not gives us amendments." "The grass withereth, the flower fadeth; but the word of God shall stand forever," says the God's word.

"Heaven and earth shall pass away but my words shall not pass away," said Jesus.

In the Bible we find exactly the strength we need for every problem and sorrow of life. For those overcome with grief over the passing of a loved one, who can offer better comfort than Jesus who is the resurrection and the life? For those overcome by the cares and burdens of life, who can offer greater strength than Jesus Who says, "Come unto me all ye that labor and are heavy laden and I will give you rest"? For those overcome by guilt, who can offer greater forgiveness, greater peace than Jesus Who said to the adulteress, "Neither do I condemn you. Go and sin no more"? For those who cannot stand the emptiness of life, who can fill it with more meaning than Jesus who said, "I am the bread of life, he who comes to me shall never hunger and he who believes in me shall never thirst"?

In the Orthodox Church we cherish the highest respect for the Bible. We keep the Gospel book enthroned on the altar constantly. Just as the Bible is enthroned on the altar of our church so it should be enthroned in the heart of every Orthodox Christian. By this we don't mean that it should be kept on some shelf at home as a magic charm. It should be opened and read daily.

How to Read the Bible

We offer the following suggestions for family Bible reading:

1. Set aside a regular time for daily reading preferably in the evening at the supper table when the whole family is together. When the children are young, mom or dad can do the reading. When the children

grow older, they may share in the reading. Reading to children is one of life's greatest joys. Children treasure it.

2. Don't read too much or too fast. One chapter a day is sufficient. Let what you read sink in slowly. If the children are young, read from a Bible story book-one that has pictures which you can show the children.

3. Start with the biographies of Jesus (Matthew, Mark, Luke, John).

4. Read with the faith and the expectation that God will really and truly speak to you through what you read.

5. Don't worry about the passages you do not under stand. Concentrate on what you do understand. The more you read, the more you will understand. One passage explains another.

6. Each day memorize at least one verse that grips you. Say it out loud as a family three or four times. Encourage your children to fall asleep with this verse on their lips.

7. Get a modern translation. The New Revised Standard* translation or The New Oxford Annotated Bible With the Apocrypha*, The Orthodox Study Bible* are highly recommended.

8. As you read, try to have an icon of Jesus before you if you are reading the Gospels; one of St. Paul if you are reading his epistles, etc. This will help you realize who it is who is speaking to you.

9. *The Golden Children's Bible* is an excellent Bible story book for children. It is beautifully illustrated in full color and simply written.*

---

* Avaialble through Light and Life Publishing Company..

Make Lent a Spiritual Spring

Man today has become a giant. Jet airplanes have given him wings to fly faster than sound. Radar has given him eyes so powerful that he can see through fog and darkness. Electronics have given him a giant ear to amplify the slightest whisper, turn it into a shout and hurl it across the world. Nuclear fission has given man powerful fists with which he can wipe out entire cities with one blow.

Unless man acquires a new giant soul to match his giant eyes, ears and fists, he will not remain a giant for long. How can man acquire a giant soul?

Perhaps the period of Lent can be of assistance to us in this respect; for Lent was always intended by the church to be a period of growth for the soul, growth in the life of Christ.

Soon the snow will melt in the northern climes. The grass will turn green. Chipmunks, toads, and frogs will awaken from their winter sleep. Tulips will bloom and the trees will be covered with buds. Earth will come alive.

What is it that will cause the earth to come alive? Spring! Of course. But what is in Spring that causes the earth to come alive? The greatest secret of Spring is the sun! Spring is the in-between period when the earth is changing its position, turning toward our great source of heat and light; the sun. Spring, then, is that time when our hemisphere simply moves into the position where the sun can bring new life.

It is significant that Lent happens to coincide with Spring in northern climes. I think there is a wonderful lesson for us in this happy coincidence. Lent should be for all of us a period of placing ourselves in the position where the best things can happen to us. That position for Orthodox Christians is the presence of Christ, where the Sun of His love and power can shine into our arid souls to bring about a real awakening, a real springtime of the soul. Lent should be for all of us a period of turning our souls toward the Source of Power and New Life through daily prayer, spiritual reading, the divine liturgy and participation in the sacraments.

The church's service book for Lent (Triodion) calls this period the "spiritual spring which blossoms with the fruits of the Spirit . . . love, joy, peace, patience, kindness, goodness, faithfulness, gentleness, self-control" (Gal. 5:22)

An African folk tale tells of a clearing made in virgin jungle. Certain ground was exposed to sunlight for the very first time. Strange shoots appeared, strange plants, with flowers of indescribable beauty. Natives had not dreamed that these exquisite plants could grow in that place. Often the same is true with us. We allow old sins and evil habits to grow to the point where our soul becomes like a jungle. But if through sincere repentance we allow Christ to forgive us, He will remove the sins that hide us from the life-giving sun of His Spirit. He will make flowers of indescribable beauty grow where formerly there were weeds. He will help us achieve our greatest potential. How?

Confession

Lent from the earliest days of Christianity was always a period of public penance-a period of self-examination, a period of clearing away the underbrush of sin to let the Sun (Son) of God's love shine on us.

Many times we become so accustomed to our way of living that we feel it is the only way to live. The doctor in *Les Miserables* spent years in the Bastille mending shoes in the darkness of his cell. When at last the Bastille fell and he was freed he found himself afraid. He was afraid to go out. So the rest of his life was spent in a darkened cell, mending shoes with the door un-locked.

This story brings to mind what St. John Chrysostom said once, "The sun may be shining in all its brightness but each one of us is free to shut it out of our lives merely by closing our eyelids." Unfortunately people can shut the sun out of their lives and become accustomed to the darkness in which they live. Like the cobbler in *Les Miserables*, they become prisoners but by their own choice. For the Sun of God's love is always shining and to let it into our lives is as simple as opening one's eyelids.

During Lent we are urged to come to ourselves, leave the darkness of sin and return to the Father. It is for this reason that the Church offers us the Sacrament of Confession. Orthodox parents should discuss this sacrament with their children and prepare to come to it with them. A very helpful booklet to prepare both parents and children for confession is Fr. Hopko's *If We Confess Our Sins*.

The Special Services of Lent

An excellent way to help our children enter into the real meaning of Lent is by attending the many special Lenten services. Foremost among these are:

a. *The Liturgy of the Pre-Sanctified Gifts.* This ancient liturgy is a living testimony from the early Church testifying to the fact that the Christian cannot live the life of Christ unless he continually re-news his union with the Source of Life, Christ, by receiving His precious Body and Blood. During the early Church, the divine liturgy was not celebrated Monday through Friday during Lent because it was joyfully paschal in character and thus, not in keeping with the somber and penitential season of Lent. St. Basil tells us that the Christians of this period had to receive Communion four times a week, i.e., Wednesday, Friday, Saturday and Sunday. In order not to deprive themselves of the Sacrament on the Wednesdays and Fridays of Lent, the Liturgy of the Pre-Sanctified Gifts was composed. It is a vesper service to which prayers from the later part of the liturgy are added. The bread and wine are consecrated at the previous Sunday's liturgy and are merely distributed at this liturgy, i.e., there is no consecration of the gifts. The Pre-Sanctified Liturgy is penitential in character. The atmosphere of the sanctuary is somber. Wearing dark vestments the priest offers prayers that are full of humility and penitence. It is one of the most mystical of all services-a service that all Orthodox families should attend together during Lent. (For the text and explanation of this liturgy, use the booklet "The Pre-Sanctified Liturgy" by the Orthodox Church in America or one recommended by your parish priest).

b. *The Akathist Hymn* is chanted on the first five Friday evenings of Lent in Greek Orthodox Churches. It is a beautiful poem enlarging upon the meaning of the angel's greeting to Mary at the Annunciation, "Hail, thou that are highly favoured" (Luke 1:28). A beautiful conversation takes place between the Virgin and the Angel on the meaning of the Incarnation. The story of the birth of Jesus is beautifully retold. The Akathist Hymn is chanted during Lent in view of the fact that the great feast of the Annunciation, which it describes, is usually observed during the Lenten period. The Akathist is the kontakion (a hymn highlighting the main theme of a feast day) of the Annunciation.

Orthodox families should attend this service with an Akathist prayer book to follow the meaning of the beautiful verses. Most churches provide such books before the service.

    c. *The Canon of St. Andrew of Crete.* This beautiful service is chanted during the first week of Great Lent and also during the fifth week. Written in the seventh century by St. Andrew, a monk of St. Sabbas monastery near Jerusalem who later became Archbishop of Crete, this inspiring canon is entirely Scriptural. It sets the tone for Lent by expressing the lament of the soul over its separation from God through sin. Between each verse of the poem the penitential refrain of the psalm is repeated: "Have mercy on me, O God, have mercy on me:"

Where shall I begin to lament my wretched life's actions?
What shall I set for first-fruits, O Christ, of this lamentation?
But grant in Thy compassion forgiveness of trespasses.
Have mercy on me, O God, have mercy on me.
Come, sorry soul, with thy flesh to the Creator of all.
Make confession and be far from thy former beastly state.
And offer to God tears of repentance.
Have mercy on me, O God, have mercy on me.
Adam, the first-formed, I rivalled in my transgressions.
Then I found myself naked, stripped bare of my God,
And of that royal unending delight because of my sins.
I cry like the harlot, I only have sinned.
I have sinned against the Saviour.
Accept now my tears like hers as the ointment.
Have mercy on me, O God, have mercy on me.
I have sinned like David and am deep in the mire,

But wash me also, O Saviour, clean with my tears.
Have mercy on me, O God, have mercy on me.
I cry like the publican: "Be merciful, Saviour!"
For none of Adam's children have sinned against Thee as I.

Orthodox families may attend the compline services during the first week of Lent where the Canon of St. Andrew of Crete is sung. The beautiful service will help set the tone for the entire season of Lent.

Fasting

Another Orthodox discipline for Lent is fasting. The Triodion tells us that Adam lost paradise because he failed to keep the fast. During Lent we are called to gain paradise by keeping the fast. For a discussion of this discipline, please refer to the chapter on fasting in this book.

For Further Reading

Parents who wish for more detailed material about Lent which they can discuss with their children are referred to the following excellent book:

Great Lent by Fr. Alexander Schmemann (highly recommended).

From the Triodion

The Lenten spring has come,
The light of repentance . . .
Let us receive the announcement of Lent with joy!

For if our forefather Adam had kept the fast,
We would not be deprived of paradise . . .
While fasting physically, brothers,
Let us also fast spiritually;
Let us loose every knot of iniquity,
Let us tear up every unrighteous bond,
Let us distribute bread to the hungry and welcome to
our homes those who have no roof over their heads
So that we may receive great mercy from Christ our
God.

Holy Week: Re-living the Last Days of Christ

For Orthodox Christians Holy Week is a "red letter week." It is the most important and significant week of the entire church year. During this week the church re-enacts before us the entire passion of Christ.

When the Orthodox Church celebrates an event in the life of our Lord, it does not simply commemorate or remember the event. It re-lives the event so that we today may experience it for ourselves. It brings the past into the present. In many ways it's like a TV program a few years ago called "You Are There", which made present again and re-lived actual historical events. It made us feel as if we were actually there.

Experience It!

In this the Orthodox Church is very much like the Jewish synagogue. When our Jewish brethren celebrate the exodus from Egypt, they re-live the event in order to experience it personally. The ancient rabbis taught, "In every generation every man should look upon himself as if he personally had experienced the exodus from Egypt. The Passover says to us, 'Don't just discuss the exodus, feel it! The experience changes your outlook on life . . .'" Thus our Jewish brethren celebrate the Passover today by eating the same unleavened bread and chewing the same bitter herbs in order that they may in some way feel for themselves the bitter plight of their fathers who were slaves in Egypt. The past is made to live in the present so that the Jewish person today may feel as if he himself were brought out of the slavery of Egypt by God.

We Orthodox Christians do the same. We try to re-live the religious event we observe on a particular day. This is why at Christmas we sing,

"*Today* Christ is born in Bethlehem of the Virgin. . ."

During Holy Week we sing:

"*Today* there stands before Pilate the Lord of Creation. . ."

"*Today* there hangs on the Cross He who has suspended the earth in the midst of the water . . ."

At no other time of the year do we have the opportunity to experience the love of Christ as much as during Holy Week which begins with the Saturday of Lazarus. It is significant that Holy Week begins with Christ resurrecting Lazarus from the dead. Lazarus, the *friend* of Jesus, personifies each one of us, for we are all friends of Jesus. With Lazarus's resurrection "death begins to tremble." Thus begins Holy Week-the decisive duel between Life and Death-a duel that will end with the final victory of Life over death on Pascha.

Palm Sunday

Then comes Palm Sunday when Jesus is acknowledged and acclaimed as the Messiah, the King and Redeemer of Israel. With palm branches in our hands we identify ourselves with the people of Jerusalem. We are there! Together with them we greet Christ and confess Him to be our King not for the few hours that we are in church but for all time and in every area of our life. With palm branches in hand we renew our baptismal vow to follow Christ as King. We signify our readiness to take up our cross and follow Him, to make Him Lord of our lives.

Following the Palm Sunday liturgy we take palms home and place them on the family icon shelf.

Services the First Three Evenings

During the services on Sunday, Monday and Tuesday evenings of Holy Week we follow Christ day by day as He cleanses the temple, answers the questions of His enemies, and gives His final teachings to His disciples. During the first service on Sunday evening the icon of Christ the Bridegroom is carried through the darkened church in solemn procession and placed in the middle of the church where it will remain until Holy Thursday. This symbolizes the condemned Christ on His way to Golgotha. At this time the following troparion or hymn is sung calling on us to prepare for His coming:

Behold the Bridegroom cometh in the midst of the night
And blessed is the servant whom he shall find watching . . .
But unworthy He whom He shall find careless.
Beware then, my soul, lest thou be weighed down by sleep,
Lest thou be given over to death
And be shut out from the Kingdom;
But awake, crying,
Holy, Holy, Holy art thou, O God
Through the Mother of God, have mercy upon us.

The three Bridegroom services are most inspiring. Children will benefit greatly by attending these services with their parents.

Holy Thursday

On Holy Thursday morning we commemorate the institution of the Sacrament of Holy Communion at the Last Supper. On this day we stand with the Lord in the Upper Room as He directs to us the same words He directed to His disciples: "Take, eat, this is my body, broken for your sins . . . Drink ye all of it this is my blood . . ." Many Orthodox Christians receive Holy Communion on this great day when the Sacrament itself was instituted. During the liturgy on Holy Thursday we sing the hymn:

Receive me today, O Son of God, as a partaker of Thy Mystic Feast . . . I will not kiss Thee as Judas, but as the thief I will confess Thee, Remember me, Lord, when Thou comest into Thy Kingdom.

On the evening of Holy Thursday twelve special Gospel lessons are read which tell the entire story of our Lord's suffering and death from His farewell talk to His disciples to His burial and the sealing of the tomb. After the fifth Gospel lesson, the large Crucifix adorned with floral wreaths and candles is carried in procession and placed in the center of the church to be venerated by the worshippers as the choir sings:

Today there hangs on the Cross He who has suspended the earth in the midst of the waters. A crown of thorns crowns Him, Who is the King of Angels. He is wrapped about with the purple of mockery, Who wrapped the Heavens with the clouds. He is struck

in the face He who freed Adam in the Jordan. He
was transfixed with nails, He Who is the Bridegroom
of the Church. He was pierced with a spear, He Who
is the Son of the Virgin. We worship thy passion, O
Christ, show us also unto thy glorious resurrection.

The icon of the Last Supper should be displayed on this day in the family icon corner. Parents can tell the story of the Last Supper and explain simply what we believe about Holy Communion (see chapter elsewhere in this book).

A foot washing service is also performed on Holy Thursday commemorating the washing of the disciples' feet by Jesus.

Good Friday

Then comes Good Friday. In the morning service the Old Testament prophecies relating to our Lord's death are read. In the afternoon we celebrate the vesper service of the unnailing of Christ from the Cross and His burial. At this service, the Body of Christ is removed from the large Crucifix which has been standing in the center of the Church since Thursday evening. It is wrapped in a clean white shroud and placed on the altar as the priest reads the Gospel account of this event. Then the icon of the *epitaphion* which represents the death and entombment of Jesus is placed in the tomb of our Lord which is adorned with flowers. In the evening, holding lighted candles, we gather round the beautifully decorated tomb of Jesus to chant a series of lamentations expressing our sorrow; our belief that He had descended to Hades to abolish the power of Satan and to trample upon death; and our expectation of His life-giving resurrection. We sing:

*Oh, life, how liest Thou dead. How dwellest Thou in
a tomb?
Oh, Christ, the Life, Thou hast been placed in a
tomb.
By Thy death Thou hast abolished death, bringing
forth joy for the world.*

At the conclusion of the service the worshippers come
forward to reverence the icon of the entombed Christ and to
receive a flower from His tomb which is taken home and kept
in the family prayer corner.

Holy Saturday

On Holy Saturday morning as we gather for the celebration of the Liturgy of St. Basil, Christ is still in the tomb. The
congregation gathers at the sealed sepulcher. Yet it is in the
light of the Resurrection that we stand before the tomb.
Already we are anticipating the Resurrection. From Ezekiel
we hear the promise, "Behold my people, I will open your
graves, and cause you to come up out of your graves." The
priest, wearing brightly colored vestments, disperses flower
petals in a procession through the church. This act serves as
the first heralding or pre-announcement of the Resurrection.
The final reading of Holy Saturday promising the resurrection: "After three days I will arise again" also notes the sealing of the tomb:

*So they went and made the sepulcher secure by seal-
ing the stone and setting a guard (Matt. 27:62-66).*

Finally, we come to the climax of Holy Week: Holy Saturday evening. As the congregation gathers, the church is still clothed in darkness. It is still Holy Saturday. The tomb remains sealed. The service begins as a funeral dirge. Suddenly, at the stroke of midnight, the old day passes into the new. A new era begins. A new age dawns. The darkness, symbolizing death, is pierced, destroyed, annihilated by hundreds of candles and by the excited, triumphant singing of *Christ is risen from the dead. By His death He has trampled upon death and to those in the tombs He has bestowed life eternal.*

Buried and Risen With Him!

Thus it is that Holy Week can be a life-changing week in the life of every Orthodox Christian. During this week we hear Christ's final words to us. We witness His betrayal. We stand with Him before Pilate. We witness His scourging. We see Him as He carries the heavy cross to Golgotha. We see the nails being driven into His hands and we realize that ours are the sins that drive those nails into His hands. It was neither the Jews nor the Romans who crucified Christ. Our sins crucified Him. So, during Holy Week, by re-living and experiencing for ourselves the Passion of Christ, we are called upon to die with Christ, to die to our lower, sinful self by true repentance and honest confession that we may rise with Christ to a new life. This is the meaning of the Easter hymn, *Yesterday, O Christ, I was buried with You; today I rise with You . . .*

Pascha is not merely an annual commemoration-solemn and beautiful-of a past event. It is also a contemporary event that can be experienced in our lives as we, too, by Christ's power rise from the tomb of slavery to freedom, weakness to power, despair to hope, doubt to faith, death to life.

Prayer By St. Tychon

O Lord, You submitted to an unjust trial-You Who are the Judge of all the earth-that I might be freed from eternal judgement. You were made naked in order to clothe me in the robes of salvation, in the garments of gladness. You were crowned with thorns that I might receive the crown of life. You were called king in mockery-You, the King of all!-to open the Kingdom of heaven for me . . . You were given vinegar to drink that I might eat and drink at the feast in Your kingdom . . . You were laid in the tomb that I might rise from the tomb. You were brought to life again that I might believe in my resurrection. You ascended into heaven in order that I too might ascend into heaven and be glorified in Your Kingdom. This You have done for me, Your servant, O my Lord!

Holy Unction: The Family Healing Service

On Wednesday of Holy Week we go to church to be anointed with the Sacrament of Holy Unction. This is one of the seven sacraments of the church. It is the sacrament for healing.

Spend a few moments at home to discuss this sacrament before you attend the service at church. Share with your children some of the information in this chapter.

The church as the house of God is a spiritual hospital to which people come with diseases of mind, soul and body. They come to the Great Physician Who touches them with His healing power. *And the whole multitude sought to touch him: for power went out of him, and healed them all*, we read in the New Testament.

Someone asked a Christian one day: "Do you believe in divine healing?" The Christian replied, "What other kind of healing is there?"

In the entrance hall to a great hospital in the United States, there stands a statue of the healing Christ. By whichever door one enters, one seems to be facing Christ, the One Who is behind all healing.

To see how the Sacrament of Unction was established, turn to the Epistle of James and read verses 14-15 in Chapter 4: "Is any among you sick? Let him call for the elders of the church (presbyters or priests), and let them pray over him, anointing him with oil in the name of the Lord, and the prayer of faith will save the sick man, and the Lord will raise him up. . . ."

The two things that are necessary for this sacrament according to St. James are (1) the anointing with oil in the name of the Lord, and (2) the prayer of faith.

The Anointing with Oil

The anointing with oil is the visible sign used for this sacrament. In the days of Jesus olive oil was considered to possess healing power. Herod the Great was bathed in it when he came to death's door. Jesus Himself related how wine and oil were poured by the Good Samaritan on the wounds of the man found by the side of the road. The oil used in the Sacrament of Unction is an external sign used to signify the healing power of God that is imparted to the believer. The oil is blessed by the Holy Spirit during the service to bring us God's healing power.

The Prayer of Faith

The second element required for the Sacrament of Unction according to St. James is "the prayer of faith." As we come to be anointed with the consecrated oil, we must bring with us our "prayer of faith," i.e., a living personal faith that when we are anointed with this oil, the hand of Christ will touch us with His healing power.

Faith is like a receptacle. The more faith we have, the more healing power God can pour into us. Where there is no faith, we must not expect miracles of healing. "Be it done to you according to your faith," said Jesus.

God speaks to us through the fourteen Scripture readings that are part of this sacrament (seven Epistle readings and seven Gospel readings). The readings are designed to increase our faith in His power to heal.

The fact that the presence of seven priests is recommended (but not required) for the celebration of this sacrament gives expression to our faith that the whole Church is present and praying for the sick person.

It is not necessary to travel to one of the great shrines such as Tinos, Lourdes, etc., for healing. Through the Sacrament of Holy Unction, every church becomes a healing shrine pervaded by the prayers of the clergy and the faithful, and hallowed by the presence of the Holy Spirit. Here we find our faith fortified and sustained as we grow in grace and understanding. Here we find the power and the presence of the healing Christ.

We should teach our children that Unction is available throughout the year. Whenever a person is ill, the priest can be invited to pray and anoint the sick person either at church or at home. Unction may also be kept at home to be used with prayer in time of illness.

The Body: A Temple

During Holy Week when we are reminded how much God suffered on the Cross to save our souls, the church does not overlook the fact that God cares also for our bodies. This is why on Holy Wednesday every year the church offers the sacrament of healing for the body.

Most pagans looked upon the body as something evil. They considered it a prison in which the soul was kept prisoner. Their whole philosophy of salvation centered in helping the soul free itself from the chains of the body through extreme fasting and self-mortification.

Christianity, on the other hand, looked upon the body not as a PRISON but as a TEMPLE of God. "Do you not know that your body is a Temple of the Holy Spirit," writes St.

Paul. God dwells in your body. Your body is a church-a living, walking church. It is destined not for the earth: "Dust thou art and unto dust shalt thou return"; it is destined for heaven. When we see Christ ascending into heaven with His physical body, we see humanity-ourselves-ascending there with Him. The body that dies is buried in a grave, but only temporarily. One day God will resurrect the buried body to dwell with Him forever. For the healing and well-being of this body-temple God has given us a special sacrament.

An Encounter with Christ

It is important that we teach our children that every sacrament is a personal encounter with Christ. When we go to be anointed on Holy Wednesday, we shall be anointed not by the priest but by Christ through the priest with His healing power. We must approach with faith, with an inner longing to be touched by our Lord Who loves us and has the answer to all our needs. We must approach with our life completely surrendered to Him. We must approach as empty cups seeking to be filled with God's healing presence. We must come with deep repentance for our sins, with a broken heart and a contrite spirit, having confessed our sins and determined by His power to forsake them. We must approach with the "prayer of faith":

Lord, touch me.
Anoint me.
Heal me.
Forgive me.
Strengthen me.
Fill me with your Holy Spirit.
Lord, make me whole. Amen.

Before Going to Church on Good Friday

Before going to services on Good Friday it is good for parents to discuss and explain to their children the meaning of the beautiful services in which they are called to participate. In order to assist parents in their explanation we offer the following highlights.

The Service of the Descent from the Cross

On the morning of Holy Friday the service of the Royal Hours is held consisting of Old Testament prophecies relating to the passion and crucifixion of Christ and their fulfillment in the New Testament. The Vespers for Great and Holy Friday are celebrated in the afternoon. During this service the final events of the life of Christ are retold: the trial, the sentencing, the scourging, the mocking, the crucifixion, the death, the descent from the cross, and the burial. As the Gospel account is read, a person, representing Joseph of Arimathea, removes the Body of Christ from the cross, wraps it in a shroud and carries it into the altar, representing the tomb.

Toward the end of this service the priest lifts a large embroidered icon depicting Christ lying in the tomb, and carries it in a procession around the church. Finally he lays it in the specially decorated symbolic tomb in the center of the church. During the procession the following hymn is sung:

The Noble Joseph, when he had taken down the most pure body from the tree, wrapped it in fine linen, and anointing it with spices, placed it in a new tomb.

It is around the symbolic tomb of Jesus, beautifully decorated with flowers, that the evening service will take place.

The Service of the Lamentation of Our Lord's Death

In John 19:25 we read, ". . . standing by the cross of Jesus were his mother, and his mother's sister, Mary the wife of Cleopas, and Mary Magdalene." Mary the Theotokos stood by the cross and watched her Son die. In the Lamentations that we sing on the evening of Great and Holy Friday, Mary expresses her feelings about her Son's death. Sharing these feelings we sing with her the Lamentations.

In most Orthodox Churches the Lamentation hymns are printed for the worshippers to follow. Make it a point to meditate prayerfully on these beautiful hymns during the service.

Passing Under the Tomb

Some Orthodox Churches observe the custom of having children pass under the symbolic tomb of Christ on Good Friday. This act is a renewal of our baptismal commitment. When we are immersed in Baptism, we die with Christ. When we are raised out of the water, we are resurrected with Him. Passing under the symbolic tomb of Christ renews our willingness to die with Christ, i.e., to deny self, take up our cross and follow Him. Falling on our knees and crawling under the tomb of Christ is an act of humility and commitment to Christ on the day when He shed His precious Blood for our salvation.

The Procession

Good Friday in the Orthodox Church commemorates not only the death and burial of Jesus but also His descent into Hades where He preached His Gospel to all those who had died before His coming. In this descent Jesus Who is the Life encountered and destroyed death. As the hymn says, *Thou hast come down to earth to save Adam, and having not found him on earth, Thou hast descended, searching him, even into Hades . . .*

The solemn procession around the church on Good Friday with the embroidered icon of the entombed Christ is not only a funeral procession: it represents also the Son of God, the Immortal One, proceeding through the darkness of Hades pre-announcing the joy of the Resurrection. During this procession the choir sings the hymn, "Holy God . . ." The procession stops a number of times for the priest to address petitions to the Lord.

The Old Testament Prophecy (Ezekiel 37:1-14)

The theme of the Resurrection is picked up in the Old Testament reading from the Prophet Ezekiel. God speaks to the prophet who is looking into a huge valley filled with the dry bones of the dead. God announces to Ezekiel that the earth is not intended to be a universal graveyard. Not death but resurrection is the ultimate destiny of man. The dry bones will hear the words of the Lord. The dead will live again. "Behold, my people, I will open your graves and cause you to come up out of the graves . . . ."

At the conclusion of the service it is customary in some churches for the worshippers to receive a flower from the beautifully decorated symbolic tomb of Christ. This is taken home and preserved reverently in the family icon corner.

In Summary

In the ancient world it was common that people should sacrifice to God. It is something completely new that God should sacrifice Himself for us. "It is only on a cross that a man dies with outstretched arms," said St. Athanasius. His arms were outstretched to demonstrate the unfathomable depth of His personal love for each one of us. All the world's embraces cannot compare in love with the outstretched arms of Christ on the Cross. He stands ready to embrace each one of us if we will yield our lives to Him in complete obedience and walk with Him daily. The response we are called to make to the Crucified Christ on Good Friday was best expressed by St. Paul when he wrote, "I have been crucified with Christ; it is no longer I who live, but Christ who lives in me; and the life I now live in the flesh I live by faith in the Son of God, who loved me and gave himself for me" (Galatians 2:20).

The words that should be prayed over and over in every Orthodox family on Good Friday are: "Jesus, Who loved me and gave Himself for me." Have each child say these words aloud adding his or her first name after each "me."

Let's Color Easter Eggs

There was a time when it was the custom for ancient people to place eggs on the graves of their loved ones. They believed that even as a little chick is born alive out of the eggshell so their loved ones and friends would be born again out of the shell of their dead bodies. The egg was a symbol of their belief in a future life.

Christianity borrowed this beautiful idea and made it the symbol of the Resurrection of Jesus. For us Christians the Easter egg represents the sealed tomb in which the Body of our Savior was placed after His Crucifixion.

There is a tradition that the custom of the Easter egg originated with Mary Magdalene who visited the Emperor of the Roman Empire after the Ascension of Christ. She greeted him with "Christ is Risen!" as she gave him a red-colored egg. She then began to proclaim the Gospel of Jesus to him using the egg as an introduction.

Originally only red was used in coloring for eggs. This signified the sacred blood of Christ which was shed for our salvation. Gradually, other colors have also come into use.

At the conclusion of the Easter liturgy, in many Orthodox Churches, colored eggs are blessed and distributed to the congregation. Thus everyone receives a personal symbol of the Resurrection of Jesus.

The members of the congregation then greet one another by striking eggs. As they do so, the one whose egg is cracked (the seal of the tomb broken) says, "Christ is Risen!" and the other replies, "Truly He is Risen!"

The eating of eggs at Easter is symbolic also of the breaking of the long Lenten and Holy Week fast since eggs are not allowed during this period. It is a custom not to allow any Easter egg to remain unbroken in order to emphasize our faith that Christ did indeed rise from the dead "by His death trampling upon death and to those in the tombs granting life everlasting."

Every Orthodox family can make coloring eggs a family project at Pascha. They can have much fun boiling and coloring them, giving them as gifts to friends and relatives, and "cracking" them with others-always remembering how beautifully this act expresses one of the basic truths of our Orthodox Christian faith: the Resurrection of our Lord and Savior!

The Easter egg expresses the message of Pascha in several ways:

1. the red color represents the blood of Jesus shed for our salvation;
2. the egg shell represents Christ's tomb;
3. the cracking of the shell represents Christ's resurrection.

Tell Them About the Glorious Paschal Liturgy

Children look forward to attending the midnight Easter liturgy. It is an exciting experience. How much more meaningful it would be if parents spent a few moments during the family hour to explain some of the highlights of this beautiful liturgy.

Following are some of the major highlights of this service.

The Darkened Church

The Church gradually sinks into total darkness, symbolizing the darkness of the tomb, the darkness of man's life without God, the darkness of despair, the darkness of meaninglessness, the darkness of evil. This is part of the darkness in which we stand-the darkness that is within us and around us. We are-all of us-threatened by this darkness. But the glorious message of Pascha is that in darkness there is light. "In him (Christ) was life, and the life was the light of men. The light shines in the darkness, and the darkness has not overcome it." This is the message we shall hear proclaimed in the Easter Gospel lesson. God's light shines in the darkness and cannot be put out. God has come into the world in Christ Jesus, has met the full force of sin and death and has won the victory. This is the heart of our Orthodox Christian faith.

The Paschal Candle

At the stroke of midnight the Paschal candle is illuminated at the altar-the candle that represents Christ the Light of the World. The door to the sanctuary swings open, representing the opening of Christ's tomb, and the priest appears holding the light representing the Resurrected Christ, "Come, receive light from the unwaning light," he sings, "and glorify Christ who has risen from the dead." The worshippers light their candles from the Paschal candle passing on the light to their neighbors until the whole church is ablaze with the new light of the Resurrection proclaiming to the world that Christ is risen, that through His Resurrection our darkness has been changed into light, our death has become life, our midnight has become dawn, a dawn of victory.

In Greece one of the most panoramic sights is to stand on a mountain and look down on a village or a great city as the people come out from church following the midnight Easter liturgy. One sees thousands of flickering flames coming out of churches and spreading to all parts of the city or countryside.

What a meaningful custom this is. Neitzche once said that Christ is still buried. We Christians-he said-keep Him buried in the sepulchres which are our churches and we will not let Him out. The beauty of the custom of taking home the lighted Easter candle is that we carry the living, resurrected Christ out of our churches and into our homes. How quickly the darkness of this world would vanish if everyone who confessed allegiance to Christ would go out into every area of life and let the light of the Resurrected Christ shine brightly and unashamedly.

The Easter Procession

In some Orthodox churches an Easter procession takes

place. At midnight, the worshippers with lighted candles, leave the church building. The procession circles the church and returns to stand before the closed doors of the church. There the resurrection of Christ is announced, followed by the Gospel lesson which tells of the empty tomb. The Easter procession is also a reminder of the original baptismal procession which brought the newly baptized from the darkness of paganism to the light of Christ, from death to life. It is an expression of the believer's own personal passover from the darkness of sin to the light and life of the Kingdom of God. The baptismal procession reaches its conclusion in the celebration of the Divine Liturgy where we meet the risen Lord as the disciples met and knew Him after the Resurrection: in the breaking of the bread.

The Easter Hymn

Upon the return of the procession to the sanctuary, the priest reads the story of the resurrection from the Gospel of St. Mark (16:1), according to which three women come to the tomb and find it empty. An angel tells them that Jesus is risen. St. Mark then writes, "They went out and fled from the tomb; for trembling and astonishment had come upon them; and they said nothing to anyone, for they were afraid." Following this reading the choir and congregation begin singing the Easter hymn, "Christ is risen from the dead; by His death He has trampled upon death, and to those in the tombs, He has bestowed life eternal." It is sung again and again in tones ever more and more triumphant, repeated to a point of ecstatic joy. Here is the true message of Christianity: the joy that our last and greatest enemy has been defeated; the joy that Christ has won for us the greatest possible victory, a cosmic victory; a victory in which we all share. "Because I live, you shall live also," said Jesus. It is a time for tears of joy and ecstasy; a time when the true meaning of Christianity is captured.

Christ is Risen

The Orthodox midnight Easter liturgy is anything but subdued. It begins in darkness and ends in brilliant light. It begins in sadness and ends in jubilation with everyone in the congregation breaking forth with the greeting, "Christ is risen" and hearing the reply, "He is risen indeed"-a greeting used by Orthodox Christians in lieu of any other for the forty days of Easter.

The Easter Icon

The icon of the Resurrected Christ is then displayed prominently in the center of the congregation. This famous icon portrays Christ literally trampling upon the gates of hell which He has lifted from their hinges and arranged in the form of a cross. He "trampled down death by His death" and gave us eternal life, says the Paschal hymn. From the interior of Hades emerge the souls of the devout of ancient time, led by Adam and Eve who, having been first to fall, are now first to be liberated. Behind them come the just patriarchs, kings, and pious fathers of the Old Testament, who have been waiting all this time for their redemption.

The Resurrection icon may be displayed at the family icon corner during the forty days of Pascha.

The Easter Candle

At the conclusion of the Easter liturgy it is customary to take the lighted Easter candle home. Some people try to keep their candle illuminated until they reach home. It is considered a good omen if one manages to do this without letting the flame go out. Several customs are attached to the bringing of the Holy Light to the family home. Most of them derive from the belief in the miraculous power of the new Light. First, the sign of the cross is traced across the threshold of the house with the flame of the candle. Sometimes this is also done to the windows and door frames. In order to keep the Holy Light in the house all year round, the candle is then used to light the small votive light burning before the family icon. During the forty days of Easter it is customary to light the Easter candles at the supper table as the family sings together the Easter hymn "Christ is risen . . ."

A beautiful Orthodox family custom is to use the Easter candle at home during the forty days following Easter (until Ascension Day). As the family sits for supper every day they can light the Easter candles and sing together the triumphant Easter hymn: "Christ is risen from the dead. By His death He has trampled upon death, and to those in the tombs He has bestowed life everlasting." This meaningful custom will bring the light and the joy of the resurrection into every Orthodox home.

Easter Baskets

Some families bring Easter baskets to church for the food blessing ceremony on Holy Saturday. The baskets contain decorated Easter eggs, Paschal bread, ham, sausage and any other such foods as were not allowed during the Lenten fast. It is a practice that celebrates the end of the long Lenten fast. The entire family may be involved in the preparation of the basket.

The Resurrection of Jesus is the cornerstone of our Orthodox Christian faith. It deserves an important place in the home life of every Orthodox Christian. The customs outlined above help give the Risen Christ a predominant place in the home.

Exchanging the Kiss of Love on Easter Sunday

The vesper service on Easter Sunday has come to be known as the "Agape" service. The reason for this is that it became customary after this service to exchange the kiss of the Resurrection or the "kiss of love" (agape) symbolizing the love of Christ among His followers.

For example, in the old days the inhabitants of the village of Pylea in Greece used to walk out of church after the Easter liturgy and wait outside in a line to be kissed by those who followed. First, they shook hands saying, "Christ is risen," and then kissed; quarrels and feuds were forgiven and forgotten in the name of Christ. They were replaced by love, compassion, forgiveness and understanding. This beautiful custom is but an acting out of that great Easter hymn of the Orthodox Church: "It is the Day of Resurrection . . . let us embrace one another. Let us speak also to those who hate us, and in the Resurrection let us forgive all things and so let us sing: 'Christ is risen . . .'"

This beautiful custom expresses the heart of Christianity which is forgiveness and love. "By this sign shall people know that you are my disciples if you have love for one another," said Jesus. Elsewhere He said, "So if you are offering your gift at the altar, and there remember that your brother has something against you, leave your gift there before the altar and go; first be reconciled to your brother, and then come and offer your gift" (Matthew 5:23-24).

Parents should discuss with their children the meaning of the beautiful Orthodox Easter custom of exchanging the kiss of love on Easter Sunday. It is a concrete expression of the true meaning of the Resurrection.

Before or after attending the Agape vespers think of a person or persons in your circle of friends or enemies to whom you may express the special love of the Risen Christ. Then, go and do it. In each Orthodox family the Easter greeting "Christ is risen" may be accompanied by the kiss of the Resurrection. It will show that the words "Christ is risen" are not an empty greeting but one that is full of the love, the forgiveness and the compassion of Christ.

How to Celebrate Pentecost at Home

Since Pentecost is the birthday of the Church, it can be celebrated at home by baking a special birthday cake and serving it as dessert. One candle may be used to represent each 100 years of the church's existence. Twenty or twenty-one candles may be used. The whole family can sing "Happy birthday" to the church and blow the candles out together.

The opportunity may be used to read and discuss the Scripture lessons that are read in Church on Pentecost (Acts 2:1-11 and John 7:37-52, 8:12).

A discussion can follow on what the church is. It is the Body of Christ through which Jesus continues to be present in the world today: to teach us, forgive us, guide us, bless us, strengthen us. After Christ ascended into heaven, He established the church to carry on His work. When we go to church on Sunday, we are going to Christ. When we support the church with our offerings, we are supporting Christ. When we listen to the church, we are listening to Christ.

The Body of Christ

The church is called the Body of Christ because just as Christ once used His physical Body to do the work of God in the world, so now He uses His mystical Body, the church.

On the long high front wall of a church that was just being completed, an artist started painting a picture of Christ, the Good Shepherd. Only the firm brush strokes outlining the head could be seen. A stranger stopped in and asked curiously, "When will the picture be finished?" A workman replied, "That picture? It is finished."

"Finished?" repeated the startled visitor. "Why all it is,

is the outline of a head. Most of it is still missing-the eyes, mouth, arms, legs and feet-the whole body is missing!"

"You won't see that on a wall," the workman replied. "The Body of Christ is the congregation of people who will be worshipping in this church. The Body of Christ is the church."

St. Paul writes, "He (Christ) is the head of the body, the Church" (Col. 1:18). St. John Chrysostom said, "Christ is the head of the body, but what can the head do without hands, without feet, without eyes, without ears, without a mouth?"

As the Head of the Body, Christ issues orders to the various members. He is the brain; the One in Whom all the fullness of God dwells bodily. What a privilege God bestows on us when He ties us so intimately with Christ and with each other as to make us constitute one Body with Him as the Head. When we meditate on this analogy, we come to look at prayer as the members of the Body (the church) reporting for duty to the Head (Christ). He continues to be present in the world today through the members of His Body.

The Holy Spirit

Finally, parents may explain that Pentecost is the day on which the Holy Spirit came to us in His fullness. On this day we kneel three times during the church service as we pray together with the priest that the same Holy Spirit Who filled the first apostles with God's presence and power may fill us today with the same power that we may experience the reality of God in our lives.

The Holy Spirit must be received daily. To achieve this, it is necessary to wait prayerfully and expectantly for Him as the apostles did before Pentecost. "All these with one accord devoted themselves to prayer . . ." (Acts 1:14). This kind of prayerful waiting is essential if we are to receive the Holy Spirit.

St. Seraphim of Sarov describes the whole purpose of the Christian life as nothing more than the receiving of the Holy Spirit:

"Prayer, fasting, vigils and all other Christian acts, however good they may be in themselves, certainly do not constitute the aim of our Christian life; they are but the indispensable means of attaining that aim. For the true aim of the Christian life is the acquisition of the Holy Spirit of God. As for fasts, vigils, prayer, almsgiving, and other good works done in the name of Christ, they are only the means of acquiring the Holy Spirit of God . . . Prayer is always possible for everyone, rich and poor, noble and simple, strong and weak, healthy and suffering, righteous and sinful. Great is the power of prayer; most of all does it bring the Spirit of God and easiest of all is it to exercise."

It has been said that St. Seraphim in the above words sums up the whole spiritual tradition of the Orthodox Church. For, what is greater than to possess the Holy Spirit? And what is easier than the means by which He comes to us: prayer?

No prayer is complete unless it includes a petition to the Holy Spirit that He come to dwell in us. Thus, through prayer every day becomes Pentecost.

This would be a good time to teach our children one of the best known and frequently used prayers of the Orthodox Church. Almost every one of our church services begins with it. It is a prayer to the Holy Spirit:

Heavenly King, Comforter, Spirit of Truth, Who art

everywhere present and fillest all things, Treasury of good gifts and Giver of Life, come and abide in us, cleanse us of all impurity, and save our souls, O Good One.

August: The Month of the Theotokos

To the Orthodox Christian August is a sacred month-a month that brings with it a feeling of intensified reverence. It is the month of the Blessed Theotokos. For on the fifteenth of August the Orthodox Church celebrates one of the most solemn feasts related to the Mother of God, namely, her repose or falling asleep.

Special prayer services are held regularly during the first fifteen days of the month. It is a period of special fasting similar to Lent. Orthodox families are invited to attend these services and to participate in the fast.

In order to help parents explain the meaning of this sacred period to their children, we propose to deal with the following two questions:

1. What do we mean by the falling asleep of the Theotokos (Mary);
2. Why, as Orthodox Christians, do we regard her above all the saints as "more honorable than the Seraphim and more glorious than the Cherubim."

Death as Birth

In commemorating her saints, the church observes not the day of their birth, but rather the day of their death. Hence the feast day of St. Basil-January 1-is the day on which St. Basil died. The reason for this, of course, is our belief that for us the day of death is our real birthday. It marks our entry into the real sphere of existence, namely, eternal and incorruptible life. And so it is for this reason that on the 15th of August we observe the falling asleep or the death of the Mother of God. We observe this feast joyfully because the

Master has proved to us that death is not the end but the beginning of life.

Her "Falling Asleep"

Sacred Tradition has given us the following account of the death of the Theotokos. As the time drew near for the Lord to draw unto Himself His earthly mother, He announced this to her through an angel three days beforehand. With haste Mary betook herself to the Mount of Olives, and there she engaged in fervent prayer. Returning to her home she began preparations for her burial.

Meanwhile, as though by a miracle, all the apostles left off preaching wherever they were and gathered at once at Gethsemane where Mary lived. Having revealed to them the reason for their strange meeting, she then consoled them in their sorrow. Then lifting her hands heavenward, she prayed for the peace of the world. She blessed the apostles, then lay back upon her pillow. Thus did she surrender her spirit into the hands of her Son and Lord. As the apostles carried the saintly body to its resting place, heavenly voices could be heard, accompanying them on the way.

Legend has it that Thomas the apostle did not arrive in time for the burial. As the others led him to Mary's tomb to view the remains of the beloved Virgin, they discovered to their astonishment that the body was gone. Thus did the belief in her bodily assumption originate. This, in brief, is the story of the feast of the Falling Asleep of the Mother of God observed on August 15.

Why Do We Honor the Theotokos?

Why do we honor the Theotokos above all the saints? St. Nicholas Cabasilas, one of the great theologians of our church, best answers this question when he writes, "The incarnation (God becoming man in the Person of Christ) was not only the work of the Father, by His power and by His spirit, but it was also the work of the will and faith of the Virgin. Without the consent of the immaculate, without the agreement of her faith, the plan was as unrealizable as it would have been without the intervention of the three divine Persons. It was only after having asked her and persuaded her that God took her for His Mother and borrowed from her the flesh that she so greatly wished to lend Him. Just as He became incarnate voluntarily, so He wished that His Mother should bear Him freely and with her full consent."

This, then, is why we honor the Virgin so greatly. It was in the person of the Virgin that humanity gave its consent to the Word becoming flesh, to God becoming man and coming to dwell among us.

The Blessed Mother said yes to God.

She said yes for all of us. And God came down to earth to live in your life and mine.

It was as if the human race were a little dark house, without light or air, locked and latched.

The wind of the Spirit had beaten on the door, rattled the windows, tapped on the dark glass, trying to get it-and yet the Spirit was outside. But one day, a woman opened the door, and the little house was swept pure and clean by the wind. Seas of light swept through it, and the light remained in it; and in that little house a Child was born and the Child was God.

The Blessed Theotokos said yes for the human race.

Each one of us must echo that yes for our own lives.

We are all asked if we will surrender what we are, our humanity, our sins, "our whole life to Christ our God" and allow Him to fill our emptiness. The surrender that is asked of us includes complete and absolute trust; it must be like Mary's surrender, without condition and without reservation.

To surrender all that we are, as we are, to the Spirit of Love in order that our lives may bear Christ into the world- that is what every Christian is asked.

Mary-the Mother of God-made this possible for us. As the first Eve led us away from God, the Second Eve (Mary) brought God to us. Her yes was for herself and for us. She said yes to God and He came to dwell in her womb. She brought God to the world. We, too, can say yes to the Highest that He may come to dwell in us so that we, in turn, may bring Him to our world today.

Do Orthodox Christians Pray to the Theotokos?

We do *not* pray *to* the Theotokos Mary. We pray only to God. We ask Mary and the saints to pray *for* us. We ask them to pray for us much as we would ask living friends to pray for us. The Theotokos and the saints are living and they are friends as members with us of the same family of God (Body of Christ). Thus we are encouraged to ask for their prayer support. *They pray with us to the Trinity.*

Was Mary's Body Taken Up to Heaven?

Although it is not a dogma (official teaching), the Orthodox Church believes that upon death, Mary's body was translated to heaven, just as was Elijah (2 Kings 2:11). The Church's official book (Horologion) states the following concerning the bodily ascension of the Theotokos:

Upon coming to the grave and not finding the ever-holy body of the Theotokos, the disciples became assuredly convinced that she ascended to heaven in the body after those days, living the same as her Son, for she was resurrected and translated from the dead.

Like her Son, Mary underwent physical death but her body, like His, was afterwards raised from the dead and taken up into heaven in body as well as soul. The resurrection of the body which all Christians await, has in her case been anticipated and is already an accomplished fact.

The Icon of the Falling Asleep of Mary

In explaining the Falling Asleep of Mary it would be helpful to show your children an icon of this feast. Paper icons may be available through your priest. On this icon you will note the body of Mary in a reclining position to represent her death. Above her, inside a radiant ray of light, is the Lord Jesus. He is surrounded by angels and is holding His Mother's soul pictured as a babe in swaddling clothes to denote her birth through death into eternal life. At the right, near the head of the Virgin, is Peter, who is weeping and censing. At the left is Paul, and on either side of the bed-like structure can be seen the other apostles weeping. On some icons of the Falling Asleep of Mary, one finds a little pagan character who tries to upset the Virgin's bier. An angel comes to smite him. The point expressed here is the argument decided at the Council of Ephesus about whether Mary was the birthgiver of the man Christ (Christotokos) or the God-man (Theotokos). The icon shows the triumph of Orthodoxy by the angel's smiting the character who would upset the Church's official teaching that Mary is the Theotokos (birthgiver of the God-man Jesus).

Explaining the Transfiguration of Jesus

The Transfiguration of Jesus is celebrated every year on August 6. Parents can prepare their children to attend the divine liturgy on this day by reading to them the Biblical account of this event in St. Matthew 17:1-9 (also Luke 9:28-36). If the children are young, the event may be read from a suitable Bible story book which has also a picture of the Transfiguration which can be shown to them.

The following story will help parents explain the real meaning of the Transfiguration. A little boy was suddenly awakened one night by a sound in his room. Upon opening his eyes he saw a shadowy figure moving about the room. It scared him and he cried out, "Who is it?" What he did not know was that it was his father who had come to close the windows in his room because it had started to rain.

Because he wanted to reassure his son and at the same time not awaken the other children, the father simply shined his flashlight, not at the boy because that would have blinded him and frightened him more . . . but at himself, on his own face.

The little boy said, "Oh, it's you, Dad," and he turned over and went back to sleep.

St. Paul writes, "God, who commanded the light to shine out of darkness, has shone in our hearts, to give the light of the knowledge of the glory of God in the face of Jesus Christ" (2 Cor. 4:6). This verse helps explain the Transfiguration of Jesus. God, Whom we cannot see, has turned the flashlight of His revelation full force into the face of Jesus. The divine nature of Jesus shines forth in all its splendor at the Transfiguration. God, Who is light, shines in the face of

Jesus with a brightness that is brighter than the sun.

The divine nature of Jesus, the fact that He is God, could not remain hidden. It burst forth at the Transfiguration. The divine light that shone through Jesus was so bright that the disciples could not bear to gaze upon it. They immediately fell to the ground to cover their faces.

The Transfiguration reminds us how much God had to empty Himself; how much He had to tone down the brightness of His divine glory when He took on human flesh and became man in Christ. The Transfiguration reveals the true Jesus, the God-man. Here we see the divine nature of Jesus shining through His human nature with all the brightness of God's glory. God's voice is heard from heaven saying, "This is my beloved Son, in Whom I am well pleased; listen to him."

Ask the children to relate from memory other incidents during which Jesus showed Himself as God. Some answers: when He performed miracles; when He was resurrected from the dead, etc.

The Divine Liturgy as a Taborian Experience

The Transfiguration, which it is believed occurred on Mt. Tabor, happens in every divine liturgy. Through the liturgy we are brought into the very presence of God. The Holy Spirit is present. He transforms our gifts of bread and wine into the very Body and Blood of Jesus. Jesus is present. Like the disciples on Mt. Tabor, we, too, fall on our faces before Him penitently expressing our unworthiness to stand in His holy presence. But we also enjoy being in His presence. Like St. Peter we say, "Lord, it is good for us to be here. If you will, let us stay here. Let us make three tents; one for you, and one for Moses, and one for Elias."

It is "good" to be with Jesus in the liturgy, to hear Him speak to us, to receive the Holy Spirit, to be ushered before the throne of God's presence, to receive Christ within us. It is the greatest "good" on earth. But we cannot "stay" there as Peter wanted to stay on Mt. Tabor. There is work to be done in the world. We must go back. We must take Christ with us to help solve the world's problems. There is no greater example of this than Jesus. Immediately after the Transfiguration He went down from Mt. Tabor to heal a sick person (Matt. 17: 14-21).

Celebrate the Birth of the Theotokos (September 8)

September 8, the Orthodox Church celebrates the Feast of the Birth of the Theotokos (Mary).

Read to your children the story of her birth from a book on the lives of the saints.

Plan a special dessert for her birthday party. As part of grace before meals a favorite hymn to the Theotokos may be sung. If your children are young and know no hymns, let them sing "Happy Birthday" to the Theotokos.

The shared family Bible reading for this day can be the Theotokos' song of praise to the Lord (the Magnificat) found in St. Luke 1:46-55.

A Discussion＊

Ask the children to name as many saints as they can remember from the icon screen and the walls of the Church. Then ask them to guess who is the greatest of all saints. The answer, of course, is the Mother of God, but as they give their answers, do not tell them they are wrong. Agree with them that St. So-and-So is great, but not the greatest.

When the answer is established, ask them why they think the Mother of God is the greatest saint (*Panayia*, i.e., the all-holy one, in Greek). Listen to their answers. Possible answers: 1. her humility. 2. her obedience to God's will, etc.

＊ The above discussion is taken from the book "80 Talks for Orthodox Young People" by A. Coniaris which we highly recommend for family discussions. Available trough Light and Life Publishing Company.

The answer on which we shall center our discussion is that her greatness lies in the fact that God chose her to bring His Son, Jesus, into the world. It is for this reason she is called the Theotokos, i.e., the Godbearer. In many Orthodox Churches she occupies the position of honor (next to Christ in the dome) on the front wall of the church. She is often depicted holding the Christ Child in an elongated, El Greco type figure, to give expression to the truth that she joined heaven (the ceiling) and the earth (the floor of the church) by bringing the God-man to us.

The name most often used for the Mother of God is Theotokos or Godbearer. She bore Jesus. She brought Him to us. Before Jesus was conceived in her body, however, He had been born in her heart. She loved Him. She lived a life of prayer each day.

When God wanted to come to us, He asked one of us, the Theotokos. The Theotokos replied in the name of all humanity, "Be it done according to Your will, i.e., Yes, Lord, come! Be with us! Be One of us! We need you! We love you!"

In a way, we, too, can be Godbearers like the Theotokos. We can bring Christ to people today. Ask the children: can you name some ways by which you can be a God-bearer by bringing Christ to people today? Listen to their answers. Here are some:

1. by loving people ("God is love");
2. by living a life of prayer;
3. by obeying Christ in all we do;
4. by speaking to others about Christ;
5. by inviting others to come to church;
6. by bringing others into the presence of Jesus through prayer, etc.

We, too, can be Godbearers. But before we can bring

Christ to others, we must have Him in our hearts and minds. He must be born in our hearts much as He was in the Theotokos even before she gave birth to Him. Ask them to share with you how we can have Christ in our hearts today. Some answers:

1. Baptism,
2. Faith,
3. Prayer,
4. Holy Communion,
5. Reading His word in the Bible.
6. Commitment, etc.

Discuss each of them.

Explaining the Feast of the Raising of the Precious Cross (September 14)

On September 14 of each year Orthodox Christians observe a great feast day dedicated to the cross: the Feast of the Raising of the Precious Cross. Let us consider this feast day as it speaks about the cross and its meaning to us.

The Feast of the Raising of the Precious Cross commemorates the discovery of the precious cross. The cross, as you may recall, remained lost for nearly four hundred years. It was discovered in the fourth century by St. Helen, St. Constantine's mother. St. John Chrysostom, in 395, speaks of the three crosses discovered by the Empress Helen beneath the mound of Golgotha: that of Christ was identified because it was found in the middle and bore the inscription.

The Feast of the King

A certain legend states that the Empress Helen did not know where on Golgotha to look for the cross. As she searched she came upon a sweet-smelling plant and decided to dig under the spot. It was there that she found the cross. From that time on, according to tradition, the plant was named *Basilikos* in Greek, basil in English, which means literally, royal, regal or "the plant of the King." Basil is often used in the religious services of the Eastern Orthodox Church. We use it, for example, for the sprinkling of holy water during religious ceremonies. It has taken the place of another plant, hyssop, which was used in the religious ceremonies of the Old Testament.

The Raising

To celebrate the discovery of the precious cross the bishop, standing on a platform in the Church of the Resurrection in Jerusalem, raised the cross as the faithful sang "Kyrie eleison." This ceremony of the *ipsosis*, or raising, was celebrated in the early church since the fourth century to commemorate the discovery and raising of the cross out of the mound on Golgotha where it lay hidden for nearly 400 years.

"Knock on Wood"

St. Cyril of Jerusalem, in 349, said, "Already the whole universe is filled with fragments of the wood of the cross." There is an interesting custom which we still practice today that dates back to this time. Most Christians at that time carried with them pieces of wood which they believed were parts of the original cross. When danger threatened, they would touch the wood, thereby signifying that by the power of God through the cross they would be able to endure. This is how the habit of "knocking on wood" to avoid danger originated. Originally it was not "knocking" on wood but touching a piece of wood which they believed to be a fragment of the cross.

In the year 628 A.D. the infidel Persians succeeded in pushing back the Byzantine armies. They captured Jerusalem, then belonging to the Christian empire. Among the booty they carried off was the very cross upon which our Lord Jesus Christ had been crucified.

The Christian Empire could not tolerate such irreverence and desecration. Fresh forces were organized to recapture Jerusalem and win back the precious cross from the pagan enemies.

The Recovery of the Cross

Under Emperor Heraclius III the Persians were repulsed and the precious cross was recovered. The victory was celebrated in a most fitting manner. The ceremony of the Raising of the Precious Cross was again performed amid great rejoicing; this time to celebrate not only its discovery by St. Helen, but also its recovery from the hands of the infidel. The chanting of the "Kyrie eleison" (Lord have mercy) arose in unison as the cross was raised once again before the adoring eyes of thousands of Christians.

This centuries-old ceremony is repeated every year on the Feast of the Precious Cross. The precious cross of Christ, surrounded by sweet-smelling basil, is first lowered to the ground, to denote that for 400 years it was buried, lost, and then it is slowly raised to commemorate its discovery by St. Helen in the fourth century and its eventual recovery from the Persians in the seventh century.

The Son of Man Was Lifted Up

But there is a deeper significance to the raising of the cross as we practice it on this day. Our Lord refers to it when He says in John 3:14, 15, ". . . as Moses lifted up the serpent in the wilderness, so must the Son of man be lifted up, that whoever believes in him may have eternal life." Jesus is referring to the time when the Israelites were in the wilderness. They were rebelling and complaining. Because of their disobedience, God sent poisonous snakes to punish them. The people were dying from the bites. They went to Moses with a protest and an appeal for help. Moses, as always, took his troubles to God. God told him to raise the standard of a brazen serpent and to tell the people to look upon it when bitten. Healing would come by looking at the standard. And it did. Those who looked at the brazen serpent were healed. Perhaps this is why the serpent today is used as an emblem of healing by medical doctors.

As Moses lifted the serpent in the wilderness, says Jesus, so must the Son of man be lifted upon the cross that whoever believes in Him might have eternal life. Thus, every year on this feast, the church raises the cross in our midst. She raises it so that we today may find healing and strength in the uplifted cross of Christ. For we, too, become infected with the deadly poison of sin and guilt. Salvation for us, too, is in a look-a look of faith, repentance and commitment to the crucified and risen Christ.

Parents will combine the above explanation with the experience of the liturgy on this day where the actual burial, discovery, recovery and raising of the Precious Cross will be enacted before them.

The sweet-smelling basil we receive on this day reminds us of the exquisite treasure we find in the Risen Christ. We take the plant home and keep it by our family icon as a constant reminder of the sweetness of salvation in Christ.

A Family Practice for Thanksgiving Day

A good family practice for Thanksgiving Day (celebrated in the U.S.A.) is to allow each family member to state what he or she is thankful for. This may be done in the form of a personal prayer by each one, i.e., "Dear Lord, thank You for . . ." After this is done, crayons and paper may be given to the children with a double suggestion: first, that they write their own personal "thank you" note to God, naming the blessings for which they are thankful; secondly, that they write and mail a thank you note or letter of appreciation to some person who helped them in some way.

Following is a list of personal testimonies of thanksgiving by various people. These may be shared with the family to show how endless our list of blessings can be.

You can always find something for which to thank God. If you have a pain in the neck, thank God you are not a giraffe!

Benjamin Franklin: "Some persons grumble because God placed thorns among roses. Why not thank God that He placed roses among thorns?"

T. J. Villers: "On our national calendar only one day is set aside for Thanksgiving . . . It would be preferable to have just one day wherein to voice our croaks and complaints, our disappointments and dissatisfactions, our grunts and growls and grumbles, and leave the other 364 days in which to bless the Lord who satisfies our mouth with good things, forgives all our iniquities, redeems our lives from destruction, and crowns us with lovingkindness and tender mercies."

Anonymous: "If you can't be thankful for what you receive, be thankful for what you escape."

Bill Gold: "I think that one of the things I'm most grateful for on Thanksgiving Day is that when the Lord was deciding who would need help at this season and who would be in a position to give help, He permitted me to be among the givers."

St. Chrysostom, the great preacher, had the curious thought that a Christian could even give thanks for hell, because hell was a threat and a warning to keep him on the straight path.

Anonymous: "If you think you're self-sufficient, remember it takes all the heavens to ripen one raspberry." When was the last time we thanked God for a raspberry?

Archbishop of York: "If God had created only one rose in the world, people would travel hundreds of miles to see it. However, God has created millions of roses and so we do not take notice of them. Likewise, if God had only given us one blessing, we would be forever thanking Him. But He has given us countless blessings, so we neglect to thank Him."

Anonymous: "If the good God makes every day a day of giving, should we not make every day a day of thanks?"

"What is the Christian life but endless striving born of gratitude? said Kierkegaard.

Famous celebrities from around the world were asked, "What do you want most?" A writer said, "Give me health." A wealthy patron wanted a zebra. A well-known citizen wanted a little Vermont farm with a brook. A prominent lawyer desired an uninterrupted day with his grandchildren. One of the most respected celebrities answered: "I would ask to be given an ever-greater ability to appreciate what I now have."

How many of us ever thank God for disease? or financial reverses? or suffering? St. Paul does! Listen: "More than that, we rejoice in our sufferings, knowing that suffering produces endurance, and endurance produces character, and character produces hope. . . ."

Ultimately, our attitude of gratitude does not depend on changing fortunes but rather in our faith in the unchanging God;

- a God Who is not in some far-away heaven seated on a glittering throne,
- a God Who stands with us in every tribulation;
- a God Who offers Himself to us in every liturgy: "Take, eat, this is my body . . .";
- a God Who shares our troubles and stands ready to turn them into ultimate victory;
- a God Who says, "Come unto Me all ye that labor and are heavy laden and I will give you rest";
- a God Who receives every penitent sinner today as He received the thief on the cross, "Today you will be with me in Paradise";
- a God Who has overcome evil for us, "In the world you have tribulation but be of good cheer, I have overcome the world";
- a God Who went down into the tomb and came back to prove that He is Lord of life and death;
- a God Who supplies "all our needs according to His riches in glory in Christ Jesus" (Phil. 4:20).
- a God Who as FATHER stands above us; as SON stands beside us; as HOLY SPIRIT lives within us;
- a God Who blessed us, chose us, adopted us, redeemed us, forgave us, remembered us in His will and sealed us with the gift of the Holy Spirit.

We do not ask today the question Jesus was asked by a lawyer: "What shall I do to inherit eternal life?" God's grace has taken care of that. Our question is much more simple: "How can I show true thanks?" The answer comes to us in the words of the greatest Christian commandment: "You shall love the Lord your God with all your heart, and with all your soul, and with all your strength, and with all your mind; and your neighbor as yourself."

The truth is that we can never pay for all the blessings God has given us. But we can love; we can share our blessing with others. And in a world where every year millions die because they do not have enough food to eat, this is our great mission as the Church of Jesus Christ.

We conclude with one person's thankfulness for bread:

Be gentle when you touch bread.
Let it not be uncared for-unwanted.
So often bread is taken for granted.
There is so much beauty in bread,
Beauty of the sun and soil,
Beauty of patient toil.
Winds and rain have carressed it.
Christ often blessed it.
Be gentle when you touch bread-and thankful too!

Advent: Preparing for His Coming Again

Advent is the 40-day period before Christmas which is devoted to preparation for the coming of the Messiah. It begins on November 15 (for those who observe the Gregorian calendar) and extends until December 25. It is a period of fasting, prayer, Scripture reading, church attendance and participation in the sacraments to enable us to capture the full meaning of Christ's coming.

A very effective way of celebrating advent in the home is through the use of the advent wreath. One can begin by purchasing a large styrofoam wreath in which there should be space for seven candles (one for each week of advent). Between the candles can be spread evergreen branches. The colors of the candles should be green, blue, gold, white, red and purple. If it is difficult to obtain colored candles, white ones may be used with the proper color ribbon tied around each.

In assembling the wreath, parents will explain the symbolism of each part. The circle (wreath) is a Christian symbol for God Who is eternal. The evergreen branches symbolize eternal life, or the life of God, of which Jesus came to make us partakers. The candles represent Christ Who is the light of the world. The color of each candle expresses something special that will be discussed each week of advent as the family celebration unfolds. One candle may be lit each week by a different member of the family.

First Sunday of Advent

The candle is green to express faith.

The service begins with the lighting of the first candle by a member of the family. As this is done, the father of the family begins the service by saying:

FATHER: The first candle reminds us of faith; the faith we have in God that He will keep His promise to send His Son.

VERSE: (to be said by a member of the family)
One Advent candle now we light
To show the coming of the light
Now hasten to our darkened sight
The light that's given from above.

SCRIPTURE: The Prophecy from Isaiah 9:2; 6-7; 40:3-5; 52:7

CAROL: "O Come, O Come Emmanuel"

PRAYER: Dear God, as the world that sat in darkness looked forward to Your coming, so we on this first Sunday of Advent light the candle of our anticipation. We eagerly desire Your coming to our souls to dispel the darkness of sin and prideful living, to ignite in us the flame of love and service to our fellow humans. Amen.

DISCUSSION: God kept His promise to send the Messiah. What other promises does God make? Does He keep them? Can you name some?

Second Sunday of Advent

The candle is blue to express hope.

The service begins with the lighting of the first two candles by a member of the family. Review what the color of the first candle signifies.

FATHER: The second candle reminds us of the hope
we have that Christ will come again this year
to bring new joy into our lives.

VERSE: Now that Advent lights are two,
Let us hasten to renew our vows
To pilgrim over field and stone
To find the Child and be at home.

SCRIPTURE: The Promise from St. Luke 1:5-31.

CAROL: "Joy to the World"

PRAYER: Come, Lord, into our joyless world.
Put a smile on our lips and a song in our
hearts. We have been sad too long. Amen.

DISCUSSION: Christ came to bring joy and to
make our joy complete. How does
He bring joy to our hearts today?
Why should the Christian be joyful?
What are you most joyful for?

Third Sunday of Advent

The candle is gold to express love.

The service begins with the lighting of the first three candles by a member of the family. Review what the colors of the first two candles signify.

FATHER: As we light the third candle let us remember
the words of St. John when he said that,
"God so loved the world that He gave His
only Son."

VERSE: Now three Advent candles burn
To promise aching hearts that yearn
Beneath open sky or in a crowded cell,

That Christ is coming with them to dwell.
SCRIPTURE: The Annunciation to the Theotokos
in St. Luke 1:26-38.
CAROL: "O Come All Ye Faithful"
PRAYER: Heavenly Father, help us to remember Your
great Gift to us at Christmas, the Gift of Your
love: Jesus. May His love possess our
hearts this Advent and flow out from us to
needy mankind. Amen.
DISCUSSION: Talk about the life of St. Nicholas
(celebrated December 6) who was
known for his great generosity in
distributing gifts and money to the
poor. He preferred to disguise himself and deliver his gifts after dark
so that no one would know who had
left them. How can we follow his
example in giving gifts to the needy
this Christmas? Read again the
chapter on A CHRISTMAS GIFT
LIST in this book.

Fourth Sunday of Advent

The candle is white to signify peace.
The service begins with the lighting of the first four can-
dles by a member of the family. Review the meaning of the
first three colors.
FATHER: The fourth candle reminds us of the Angel's
message to the shepherds,
"Peace on earth and goodwill toward men."
VERSE: Four Advent candles burn.

Now we with Wise Men turn
To seek the Child Who brings us light
And follow Him where'er He goes
In blazing sun or blackest night.

SCRIPTURE: The Journey to Bethlehem in St. Luke 2:1-18.

CAROL: "O Little Town of Bethlehem"

PRAYER: Christ, You are our Peace. You broke down the wall of partition that separated us from God. Now there is no condemnation for those who are in Christ. Make us reconcilers and peacemakers. Amen.

DISCUSSION: Is there someone who has some thing against us? Do we have some thing against anyone? What relationships in our lives need repairing? Whom do we need to forgive? The Prince of Peace is coming. Prepare the way. Forgive and be forgiven.

Fifth Sunday of Advent

The candle is purple to signify repentance.

The service begins with the lighting of the first five candles by a member of the family. Review the meaning of the last four candles, i.e., faith, hope, love and peace.

FATHER: The fifth candle reminds us of our need to repent before we can meet the coming of Christ. "Repent, for the kingdom of God is at hand."

SCRIPTURE: Preparing the way for the coming of the Messiah through repentance (St. Mark 1:1-8, 14 and 15).

PRAYER: Lord, help us make straight the way for You to come to us this Christmas. Grant us Your grace that we may smooth out the ruts of sin and remove the roadblocks of pride. Give us the second baptism, the baptism of tears, that we may return to You and, embraced like the Prodigal Son, be restored to full Sonship. Amen.

DISCUSSION: Discuss the meaning of repentance. Then let us prepare ourselves with a thorough self-examination and agree on a time to go to confession as a family.

Sixth Sunday of Advent

The candle is red to signify Holy Communion.

The service begins with the lighting of the six candles. Review the meaning of the last five, i.e., faith, hope, love, peace and repentance.

FATHER: The sixth candle reminds us that Christ, Who came in Bethlehem and Who will come again at the end of time, comes to us now in the great Sacrament of His Presence, i.e., Holy Communion. The reason He was born in Bethlehem was that we might allow Him to come and be born in the manger of our hearts.

SCRIPTURE: The Coming of the Logos (St. John

1:1-18). His coming today in the
Eucharist (St. John 6:52-58).

PRAYER: Lord, we thank You that You not only came
in Bethlehem but that You continue to come
in every Eucharist. Amen.

DISCUSSION: Talk about Holy Communion. Refer
to the chapters on Holy Communion
and the liturgy in this book.
How can we best prepare for
Communion?

Seventh Sunday of Advent

This service is suggested for use in the home by the family either on Christmas Eve or Christmas Day.

The candle for this service can be the same one used at the midnight Easter liturgy: the Paschal Candle representing Christ.

The service begins with the lighting of all seven candles. Review the meaning of the first six candles, i.e., faith (God keeps His promises), hope, love, peace, repentance and Emmanuel (God with us) in Holy Communion.

FATHER: "For unto us a child is born, unto us a Son is
given and His name shall be called wonderful."

VERSE: Candles at Christmas!
Deep in their warming light
Are shepherds' fires, a guiding star at night.
The holy radiance of a Baby's Birth
The Christ, Who brought the light of God to
earth.

SCRIPTURE: The Christmas Story in St. Luke 2:1-

7.

CAROL: "Hark, the Herald Angels Sing"

PRAYER: Dear Lord, today the hopes and aspirations of all the years find their fulfillment in Your Coming. You came to be the Bread of Life, the Light of the World, the Water of Life which, if any one drinks, he shall never thirst again, the Way, the Truth, the Life, our Joy, our Peace, the Good Shepherd, the Door to God's love, our Refuge, our Strength, our Redeemer and Friend. We celebrate and rejoice in Your coming. Amen.

DISCUSSION: Talk about the meaning of Christ's coming. Ask each person to share what Christ's coming means to him/her personally. For a more extensive discussion of the meaning of Christ's coming see pp. 102-121 in "Orthodoxy: A Creed for Today" by A. Coniaris.

A Christmas Gift List

A little girl was saying her prayers a few nights before Christmas. She stopped suddenly and asked her mother a question. She asked with a worried look, "What are we giving to God for Christmas? After all, it's His birthday isn't it? What does God want for Christmas?"

At Christmas we often prepare a gift list. Such a list includes parents, grandparents and favorite friends. One Person we sometimes forget is Jesus, even though Christmas is His birthday. What would you think if someone planned a birthday party for you and everyone received a gift but you?

One reason for bringing gifts to Jesus is that He first gave a gift to us. He didn't stop with a little gift, but He gave all He had-Himself. The Bible says: "Though He was rich, yet for your sake He became poor, so that by His poverty you might become rich."

Why not discuss your Christmas list with your children? What gift or gifts can you give Jesus at Christmas? One Sunday school class took a poll and found they were spending 25 hours a week watching TV and an average of only one hour a week in daily prayer, church, Sunday school and reading the Bible. Can we give Him more time? How?

What are some of the best gifts we can give Jesus? Is love a gift? repentance? obedience to His will? helping someone in need? visiting a lonely person or a shut-in? What special gift can we give Jesus as a family this Christmas?

We share with you below what one family did for Jesus at Christmas.

A pastor tells of spending Christmas Eve with a family in Illinois. After the Christmas Eve service in church the family gathered around the Christmas tree and opened their gifts.

When all the gifts had been opened, the mother said to her three sons-all in their early teens-"Now I want each of you to select the best gift, the gift you like the most."

As each lad made his selection she nodded her head in approval and directed, "Wrap it in new paper and tie it with a new ribbon."

When this had been done, she further directed, "Now write the name and address of some less fortunate boy in our congregation on the package."

Again, the boys complied.

Then, turning to the pastor, she said, "Now, Pastor, you must deliver these packages to the three persons named. Don't tell anyone who sent them. Just deliver them, please."

Surprisingly, the boys didn't grumble or argue-even though this was the first time their mother had ever taken such an action.

Years later the pastor met one of those boys-now a young man in college-who recalled that Christmas Eve. He said, "It was one of the most dramatic experiences I've ever had. That event caused me to understand in a small way what it must have cost God to give His best gift."

Godparents Sunday*

Some Orthodox priests have instituted a marvelous practice that promises to help strengthen the bond between godparent and godchild.

One Sunday each year is set aside as Godparents' Sunday. On this day the godparent invites his/her godchild to church. They sit together. They receive Christ together in the Sacrament of Holy Communion. When coming for Communion, the godchild may carry the white baptismal candle. On this day the priest usually preaches a sermon on the meaning of baptism for the Christian.

A reaffirmation of the baptismal vows may also take place on this Sunday at the discretion of the parish priest. This will afford the godchild the opportunity to confess his/her faith in Christ publicly and personally as a mature Orthodox Christian. A conscious commitment may thus be made to follow Christ as Lord and God.

Following the liturgy, the godparent may take the child out to dinner, spending part of the afternoon with him.

Parents may present this plan to their parish priest with the request that it be implemented, if possible. It affords an excellent opportunity for the godparent-godchild relationship to be strengthened. It also contributes to a fuller and more complete understanding of what Christ did for us when we were baptized.

---

* We are indebted to Fr. Angelo Kasemeotes of blessed memory for introducing us to this practice.

Godparenting

Godparenting is part of our Orthodox Christian tradition, but, like family prayer, it has been all but abandoned in its deeper implications. Godparents are not doing what they are primarily called to do, i.e., assist with the religious upbringing of the child. Yet the concept of godparenting has enormous potential for transmitting Christian values to our children. Let me say here that grandparents can also exercise an excellent godparenting ministry. The babushkas in the old USSR proved this. Stalin said once, "When the babushkas of Russia die, the Church will die." But the truth of the matter is that the babushka never did die. Stalin died. Communism died. But not the Church. Serving as godparents, the grandmothers of Russia passed the faith on to their grandchildren. As contemporary apostles they fulfilled their true priesthood by building a world of faith in the anti-God world.

Let me share with you the example of how one person fulfills her role as godparent in a rather novel way. She does it by writing letters regularly to her goddaughter who lives in a distant city. She explains how she does this:

Letters are a wonderful way to express your faith thoughtfully. A pattern of writing regularly gives the child something to look forward to. I write to my goddaughter about God and Jesus, prayer, moral discernment, sin, death (when her grandfather died) and the need for times of quiet and reflection to listen for God. Sometimes I write about the liturgical season, a special feast or biblical characters and stories; sometimes I suggest projects in preparation for a holiday. She keeps my letters in a folder and rereads them when she says her evening prayers and reads her Bible. Inviting a child to send back pictures of her favorite biblical stories or characters and eventually to write return letters brings the relationship to a level of mutuality that dignifies the child.

In truth, if we are to overcome the hostile pressures of today's godless society, it will take an entire village to raise a child, i.e., father, mother, grandfather, grandmother, godparents, church school teachers, vacation church school teachers, summer camp counselors, priests, friends, relatives, and the entire congregation. All baptized Christians-not just priests-are responsible for forming our children in Christ. Becoming a Christian was never a one-shot deal but a process, with baptism as a beginning and not as an end. To accomplish this task, we need the church, the family, and the extended family to help the baptized person become conscious of what the Holy Spirit has started in him or her and to continue the nurturing process.

Following is a letter a godparent sent to her godchild:

Dearest Mary,
Today God has chosen you to be a part of His family. Through your baptism, our Lord has come to you in the water and has declared that you are to be His child and that He will be your God. A greater day than this there shall never be for you, because today you have become one of God's saints.
As you grow in years, you will be assaulted on all sides by people who will want to change your faith in the God who has chosen you today. There

will be unbelieving people who will tell you that God does not exist or that He has abandoned the world and left us to fend for ourselves. There also will be people who strongly profess Christianity and who try to persuade you that you must accept God into your life—as if you had never known Him or had ever been accepted by Him. They will urge God upon you as though He were some product that you must possess before any of His mighty acts become effective for you.

Our dear Mary, because of what has happened in your life today, you will be able to tell these people: "God does exist, and He has shown Himself to me by coming to me in my baptism and graciously claiming me as His own."

Rejoice and be glad, Mary, for God has promised to love you always. Each day of your life, He will be with you through prayer and through the sacraments of His Church. So we pray that God's Spirit will guide you as you grow in faith and live in hope.

Your Godparent.

Who Sits In the Bleachers?

An old timer looked back to his childhood years and said,

We grew up with the strength of the tribe. If anyone were to attack me, he'd have to take on all my uncles and aunts. Families were secure. I had bleachers all around me, filled not only with family but with all the grownups in the township, cheering me on when I did well and groaning when I failed . . .

All sorts of young people today run the race with only silence from the bleachers. It's a lonely race. Grandparents are a thousand miles away, uncles and aunts scattered to both coasts and overseas, parents often busy with double jobs, harried by their own affluence, or casualties of the divorce courts . . .

If there ever was a time when society needed parents who, for the sake of their children, would forget about their own self-fulfillment and look to the higher claims of their children's right to love and safety, it is now. Now, when the world of uncles and aunts and grandparents is largely gone. If God is to reach children with the comfort they so desperately need, parents will have to be His agents. All our YMCAs and YWCAs, all our schools, all our community clubs, cannot possibly fill the bleachers reserved for parents . . .

St. Paul says that the saints in heaven are in the bleachers, constantly cheering us on to gain the crown of life. For our children, those invisible saints need to become a very visible cheering section in the bleachers, consisting ideally not just of parents but also of the rest of the body of Christ-all of us in the local parish. For are we not all members of the same family of God? the same Body of Christ? There is not one of us who cannot play an important role as a member of that cheering section in the bleachers for our children and young adults. Pause for a moment and consider the many ways in which you as a family and congregation can serve as a "cheering section in the bleachers" for the children and young adults in your parish! In your family!

When You Take Your Child To Church

Taking your child to church for the liturgy is an excellent time to teach many of the great truths of our Orthodox Christian faith.

This is an excellent time, for example, to talk about what the liturgy is. For more information about this, see the chapter on the liturgy in this book.

Upon entering the church, the parent may explain why in Greek Orthodox churches it is customary to light a candle. As both light a candle, the parent will explain that we light a candle to remind ourselves of Jesus Who is the light of the world. We received His light when we were baptized and we walk through life with it. It illumines our path and shows us the way to salvation and fulfillment.

As the parent kisses the icon of Christ in the narthex, the parent may lift the child to kiss the icon. This will be an opportunity to explain the meaning of icons in the Orthodox Church. (See special chapter on icons in this book)

Parents should limit themselves to the explanation of only one symbol each Sunday so as not to confuse the child by offering too much at once. Such explanations should be geared to the child's ability to comprehend. The Orthodox Church is so full of visual aids in its architecture, iconography, liturgy, and sacraments that there will be ample time over a period of years to talk about each symbol.

Some of the practices that can be explained are:
1. What is Holy Communion? (Consult proper chapter in this book.)
2. Why do we receive it?
3. Why and when do we make the sign of the cross during the liturgy? etc.

Religious educators keep telling us to put the means of grace into the hands of our children. In the Orthodox Church, the means of grace, i.e., icons, candles, Bibles, etc. are already in their hands and before their eyes. We need to explain to them what they mean.

For Further Reading

Let's Take a Walk Through our Orthodox Church by Anthony M. Coniaris. Light and Life Publishing Company.

Adopt A Shut-in

To help teach our children compassion for others who are in need, we suggest that a family adopt a shut-in. To implement this, you may phone your priest. Ask him if he knows of a shut-in who does not have a family to visit him. After visiting this person, secure a picture of him if possible and place it on your bulletin board at home. Let the children know as much as possible about the person: what he/she did in the church when he/she was able to be active, etc. Decide on how often you would like to visit the shut-in. We suggest that a visit be made at least monthly, and also on his/her name-day, birthday, Christmas, Easter, Thanksgiving, etc. Each child can be encouraged to make or purchase his/her own personal gift for the shut-in during the year. The whole family can work on preparing a Thanksgiving or Christmas basket and bringing it to the nursing home.

The purpose of this project is to help children make real the love of Christ to those who are lonely and neglected; to help them experience the joy of sharing their God-given gifts with others; to help them express their thanks to God for His goodness and love.

A noted family life expert says,

Lack of responsibility is a real problem. The uselessness of childhood in America is a real fact. We don't let our children do anything important. Maybe they take out the garbage, but that's it. They're useless because we have made them useless. They have no experience in being responsible for other human beings.

Our children need to have a mission in life other than to be successful, earn money and buy things. The essence of our Orthodox Christian faith is in loving, in caring, in serving others. This is what "the liturgy after the liturgy" is all about. This is why family service projects such as adopting a shut-in are important expressions of our faith.

Television: A Door Into Your Home

Dr. Margaret Mead, an anthropologist, said, "This is the first generation who have been brought up by the mass media instead of by parents."

A psychologist called TV "a sorcerer that snatches children away from their parents for three or four hours a day, which would add up to 22,000 hours by age 18." Parents, he said, use TV as a babysitter and pacifier all too often. A harassed mother, for example, urges a troublesome child to get out of her way and watch TV. Little attention, if any, is paid to the kind of program the child watches. The result is that the child's mind from the earliest and most sensitive period of its life is filled with all kinds of ideas from the tube-not too many of them good. And the children reach adolescence complete strangers to their dismayed parents.

In Chicago alone it was discovered that in the course of one week, on TV shows for children from a preschool age to the third grade, the following crimes were seen on the screen:

93 murders	33 sluggings
78 shootings	2 knifings
9 kidnappings	2 whip lashings
9 robberies	2 poisonings
44 gunfights	2 bombings

What To Do?

In view of all this and in view of the tremendous importance television has come to occupy in our lives, what should our attitude as Orthodox Christian parents be toward this medium?

First of all, we must realize that the 21-inch screen is like a door into our home. As Christians we should not allow just anything to come in through that door, especially when children are watching. We keep a screen on our windows and doors to keep out the bugs but to let in the fresh air. A similar screen is needed for our television sets. In the old days there were bad movies but children had to go to them and pay admission to see them. Now television brings murders and violence right into our living rooms.

To quote Dr. Margaret Mead again:

"We are showing our youngsters exactly the opposite of what we want them to imitate. We are showing them men who brutally attack others when angry. We show people who murder because of hatred or expediency. We show that love is expressed only by hunger for another's body. And we show them little else!"

No Time Left

Another danger of too much television is that so much time is spent before the picture tube that there is no time left for some of the truly great experiences of life, no time for the family, no time for husband and wife to sit down and talk to each other about their daily joys as well as their daily anxieties, fears, and problems; no time for family prayer, no time for storytelling, no time for Bible reading. Someone said that television is an appliance which changes children from irresistible forces into immovable objects! How true this is! If the family eats from trays in the living room, all eyes are glued to the television set, there is no conversation. It's as if you were sitting in a morgue. If the family is in the dining room, several members may be in "tilt" position so they can watch the melodrama of an old movie in the next room. The family as a unit suffers from all this. There is no longer the give and take of the past. The television schedule intrudes to split the family, to prevent communication, to cause misunderstandings, anger and loneliness.

We are not condemning television. Some of the programs on television are inspiring and educational. Many shows are wholesome and relaxing for the whole family to watch. TV can open the windows of the whole world for children. It can open their minds. Today's TV children know more about the world by the time they're in long pants than we learned all through school. And television has contributed a great deal to this increased knowledge. Some TV programs should be viewed by the entire family and discussed.

We are not condemning television as a whole just as we do not condemn movies as a whole. But we are saying that there are some television programs-just as there are some movies-that are unfit for children-and even adults to see.

Be Selective

What are we to do? For one thing, mothers and fathers should make it their business to know what their children are watching on television and at the movies, and rule out shows that are not morally good for them. Most of the people who make movies and television programs are not interested in children. They are interested only in making money at whatever expense to public decency. Fathers and mothers, who are responsible to God for the well-being of their children, must be interested. Theirs must be the task of selecting the television programs and movies their children will see. Censorship, like charity, begins at home.

Most of us would be angered if the attendant poured inferior oil into the crank case of our car, or unstrained gas into the gas tank; we happen to value our cars. Are we going to take no interest at all in what is poured into the eternal souls of our children?

We are concerned. We ought to be concerned. For our children sit by the TV set by the hour. We are allowing their tender minds to be shaped more by the picture tube and the movie screen than by us-the parents.

The U.S. Surgeon General threw his support to National TV Turnoff Week, a little noticed annual effort to wean people off excessive tube-watching, which, he says, "increases obesity, stifles creativity and shortens attention spans among young people." Children watch TV twice the amount of time they spend in school. So who is teaching your children? Every Thursday evening, for example, TV is blacked out in Iceland. There is absolutely nothing on TV. This is done deliberately by the government to give people time for other things. Is not this an example we can follow in our homes? It is certainly a good way to carve out time for family communication and family prayer, family storytelling, etc. In advocating such a blackout, we are not emphasizing renunciation, but the great pleasure that comes when we turn off the TV and rejoin the living world.

Tell Them About Sex

One of the most difficult things for parents to do is to speak to their children about sex. Because Christian parents and the church have been silent on this subject, we have allowed the world to step in and do all the talking. The result is that we are faced today with a society that gives us a totally depraved picture of sex.

Yet sex was created by God. If anyone has a right to speak on this subject with authority it is God. He created mankind as male and female. God looked upon all that He created and saw that it was very good. And God commanded that for this reason a man should cleave to his wife, and they should become one flesh. Yet we have censored God on this subject and have allowed only the devil to speak.

When parents remain silent on this subject, they literally allow the devil to speak to their children through the world, through the movies and TV. The result is that children grow up with ideas about sex that are sinful and warped.

Interfaith Statement on Sex Education

A few years ago the Greek Orthodox Archdiocese adopted the following interfaith statement about the home's responsibility in sex education:

Responsibility for sex education belongs primarily to the child's parents or guardians. A home permeated by justice and love is the seedbed of sound sexual development among all family members. Both the attitudes and the activities of the parents-toward each other and toward each child as an individual-

affect their development. Healthy attitudes toward sex begin in the child's earliest years; they can best develop in an atmosphere that fosters in him a deep sense of his own self worth, bolstered by love and understanding . . .

The Best Source

The best source of information for sex education is the home. Oftentimes one of the most misleading is the peer group. Yet most sex information is received from the peer group. Surely most Christian parents can present a more wholesome picture of sex than what is given in alleys, in garages and behind barns. The problem with most parents, however, is that they feel inadequate. "What can I say?" they ask.

Following are some things parents can say and do:

1. Let the children know that the entire body is good. St. Paul calls the body "a temple of the Holy Spirit." All of its parts and functions play important roles. No part of the body is to be viewed with disgust.

2. Create an atmosphere at home where sex questions are as natural as any other types of questions. Let it be known that sex can be discussed naturally and properly in the living room or around the dinner table.

3. Let your children know that the commandments relating to sex in the Bible are there not to give us the impression that sex is evil. On the contrary, the commandments are like a fence that God builds around sex to protect it because it is so sacred. All precious things in life are protected.

4. If a new baby is expected in your family or your neighbor's, talk about it. Explain that mom is not getting fat, but her body is getting larger to accommodate the growing baby inside.

5. Talk about changes in the body brought about by puberty. For example, when a girl experiences her first period, explain that this is a marvelous process created by God to prepare her for child bearing. Celebrate the fact that she is now becoming a woman by baking a cake, etc.

6. Christian sex standards taught in a rigid, unloving atmosphere by domineering parents are not accepted by children. Be kind and loving-the type of parent who commands your child's respect.

Telling the Story of Life

The child can be told the story of how life originates in the following natural manner:

1. Life, as we know it, comes from cells (tiny bits of living matter).

2. Babies start growing when a special father cell and a special mother cell meet in the mother's body.

3. This father cell enters the mother's body and meets the mother cell when father's and mother's love brings them very close to each other.

4. The baby grows in a safe and special place in mother's body.

5. When the baby is large enough and strong enough to live in the world, the opening in the mother's body enlarges so the baby can be born.

6. This is a wonderful story and any time you want to

know more about it ask mommy or daddy.*

A recent report concerning teenagers tells what they expect to hear from their parents on the issue of sex:
1. Teenagers want to know adults' values about sexual behavior.
2. Teenagers do not resent adults who communicate sexual standards.
3. When parents communicate clear standards and expectations, adolescent sexual activity is reduced.
4. When schools and churches help students learn how to say "no" to peer pressure, rates of sexual activity decrease.

In speaking to young people about sex I usually tell them, "Let me show you the manufacturer's manual on sex." And I show them a copy of the Bible.

Some years ago, Mother Teresa spoke at one of the prestigious Eastern secular women's colleges-a campus that had consistently been on the forefront of "free thinking" liberal education. Toward the close of her remarks, she switched gears to the topic of sexual purity, stressing the values of the Christian gospel. She issued a call to these college women to commit themselves to virginity until marriage-and she received a standing ovation! The fact is, the lion's share of our kids want to hear it the way it is.

---

* I am indebted for this explanation to Dr. Wayne J. Anderson and his book "Design for Family Living," Denison Press, a book we highly recommend.

Love Is Kind Especially at Home

St. Paul tells us that one of the characteristics of love is that it is kind (I Cor. 13:4). If love is kind, its kindness should shine forth in all its tender beauty especially at home. For this is the place where we live with the persons who are nearest and dearest to us.

Yet, the opposite is often what happens. We treat our visitors and guests at home with the greatest kindness. If one of them spills coffee on the carpet, it is promptly excused: "Don't worry! It can happen to anyone! It's just an old rug anyway. And, besides, coffee doesn't stain."

But if one of our children does the same they are usually given a tongue lashing: "You clumsy idiot! Can't you ever do anything right? Don't you have any sense at all? Can't you ever pick up anything without dropping it?"

Examine for a moment how dad treats his customers at work. No matter what they do or say, they are always right. He tries never to lose his temper with them for fear of losing a sale. He uses a very soft, pleasant tone of voice when speaking to them. He is always kind and ingratiating.

But watch out when he comes home! You wouldn't believe he is the same person. The whole attitude changes: the tone of voice becomes harsh; the temper flares; the words are caustic. He becomes like a roaring lion.

If we would only treat our children with the same kindness and consideration with which we treat our guests and customers, how different our homes would be! How happy! How pleasant! How full of happy memories!

Do we not speak of our children as little gifts from God? Do we not speak of them as brief visitors from heaven in our household? Why not treat them as such?

Children are a *reflection* of their parents if they love them and a *reaction* to them if they hate them. Treating our children unkindly builds up hatred that eventually leads to rebellion. Treating them kindly, on the other hand, exemplifies the love of God so that when they pray "Our Father, Who art in heaven . . ." the image of God as Father will be for them a pleasing and attractive one.

Remember, "love is kind" especially at home, to those nearest and dearest to us!

Teaching Our Children Values

Two social scientists who have studied American youth for 25 years, Thomas and Irene Strommen (in their book *Five Cries of Parents*) emphasize the importance of parents as communicators of values. They write,

> *Can parents make a moral difference in today's world? Our evidence says yes. Parents can remain the prime communicators of values to children. Children can adopt what their parents value and believe-if their parents have clear values and communicate them.*

Here are some vital questions we as parents ought to be asking ourselves:

1. Does my child experience from me God's love, tenderness, and forgiveness?
2. Does my child hear me talking about the Lord as I consistently include him in my thoughts and plans?
3. Does my child see me turn to Jesus for help when I am frightened, anxious or disturbed?
4. Does my child see me reading the Bible?-receiving the Eucharist regularly?
5. Does my child see and hear me pray each day?
6. Does my child see evidence of my faith in God as I trust Him for daily needs and direction?
7. Does my child see me express genuine appreciation and joy to God for his goodness?

These two outstanding Christian sociologists have found

that parents play an enormous role in the behavior of their children. Let me share with you some of their findings: "Adolescents who enjoy a close family are most likely to refrain from drug use, premarital sexual activity, and other antisocial . . . behavior. They are also the most likely to adopt high moral standards. . ." Family closeness is the key! And the Strommens have discovered that family closeness is encouraged by four elements:

1. Parental harmony; parents who love each other, get along with each other, and forgive each other.
2. Good family communication, and this doesn't come easy. We have to carve out time for it.
3. Authoritative type of parental control, where parents set the standard, always being careful as parental to speak the truth in love.
4. Parents who express love and trust in their children with words such as: "I love you. I am proud of you."

One young man in the Strommen study said, "What made me decide against something I knew was wrong were the expectations of my folks. I respect and care for them and did not want to do something I knew would hurt them."

Sharing Our Convictions

How can parents teach moral beliefs in a constructive way? Simply by sharing their convictions. One adolescent in the study said, "I feel my parents were so afraid to step on our rights as individuals that they never told us how they felt about moral decisions or problems we had to face." He wished that his parents had expressed their moral convictions. But, because they did not, he felt isolated and cut off from them. Said another adolescent: "A parent should let us know when we are off track. It's true that most of the time we need freedom to decide what we should do in a given situation. But a parent has to warn an adolescent about some dangers. Otherwise he or she might realize it when it's too late."

Another effective approach in helping adolescents internalize moral values relies on family discussions in which parents explain why certain moral values are important to them. Yet most Christian parents do not talk about values with their children. When it comes to values most parents are silent. Children need to hear their parents saying, "As Orthodox Christians, this is what we believe about drugs. This is what we believe about sex. Your body is a temple of God. It is not to be polluted with drugs or sexual impurity. These are our God-given values as Orthodox Christians. And your mom and day pray you will follow them as we try to." Some families not only talk about values but sit down with their children and draw up a list of the values they consider most crucial. They encourage their children to memorize these values-and, some even reward them for memorizing them. They talk about them and ask questions about them.

Sermons We Preach As Parents

One day, St. Francis of Assisi said to a monk in a country monastery, "We're going into town to preach today." They walked along the country road into the city, through the city, out of the city, and back to the monastery again.

The monk turned to St. Francis and said, "I thought we were going to preach today!"

"We did! We preached as we walked," replied St. Francis.

Every person preaches a sermon as he walks through life. The sermons we preach by our example and influence are far more effective than the sermons that come from the pulpit. It is a solemn thought that our lives are continually either radiating light or setting up impulses toward evil, and these are ripples of influence we can never control or stop.

Think of the sermons parents preach to their children by their daily example. The child steals a lollipop and gets a spanking. Then he washes his hands and dries them on a Hilton towel! Think of the lessons children learn by watching adults.

Think of the sermons we Christians preach to our neighbors. Henry Drummond, that great Scottish professor, gives us the story of how the Unbelievers' Club was founded in Glasgow. Some men were standing at the corner of a street when a very prosperous looking man walked past. Said one of the men, "That is the founder of the Unbelievers' Club in Glasgow." "What do you mean by that?" asked one of the men. "Why, that man is an elder of the church." "Elder or no elder," replied the man, "he is the founder of Glasgow's Unbelievers' Club." Then he told how the man's inconsistent, hypocritical life had been for years bearing such false witness to Christ that it had undermined the faith of several young men who had joined together to form the Unbelievers' Club.

Think of the sermons we preach every day as we walk through life. No man is an island. Consciously or unconsciously people are influenced by our example.

An Indian student said to a missionary one day, "We sometimes get tired of hearing about Christ. But, sir, we never get tired of seeing Christ in a Christlike person!"

Recent Research on Fathers

Recent research has shown that the manner in which a father practices his faith has the greatest influence on a child. In one congregation a study showed that where fathers worshipped with their children, 85% remained faithful to the church, and where the child participated with no interest by the parents, only 15% remained faithful to the church.

If a child sits next to his father in worship, he catches something that will never depart. The hour of worship is where a deep sense of reverence and respect can be experienced. If we complain that children have no respect for God, the place to look is at ourselves as parents. An ounce of mother or father is worth a ton of priest.

Do our children see the Gospel of Jesus in our lives? Do we treat each other with love and respect? If we do not, do we forgive each other quickly? Do we pray together as a family? Do we encourage children to make up prayers at mealtime? Do we participate regularly in the liturgy and the sacraments? Do we read the Bible regularly as a family? Do we parents try to grow in the understanding of our faith?

After being kidnapped by leftists, Claude Fly, an agriculturalist serving as a consultant in a third world nation, was asked upon his release, "What helped to sustain you through the imprisonment?"

His answer was: "The guidelines came from my father, as he nightly led the family in reading the Bible aloud and in family prayer, and as he daily lived by the Good Book, admonishing us as children to learn right from wrong, to strive to live a Christian life."

When asked how she was able to raise seven marvelous children, a Christian mother replied that her only secret was to live before them exactly the kind of life she wanted them to live.

Godparents were meant to assume the religious education of the child they baptized only in case both parents were martyred (as in the persecution of Nero). They were never meant to take over what is primarily the responsibility of parents: the nurturing of their child in Christ. All parents are godparents of their own children. They are the primary priests and preachers. The sermons they preach remain indelible.

An old schoolmaster always bowed gravely before his class before he taught them. When he was asked why, he said, "Because you never know what one of these lads may turn out to be."

When You Thought I Wasn't Looking

When you thought I wasn't looking, I saw you hang my first painting on the refrigerator, and I wanted to paint another one,
When you thought I wasn't looking, I saw you feed a strange cat, and I thought it was good to be kind to animals.

When you thought I wasn't looking, I saw you make my favorite cake just for me, and I knew that little things are special things.

When you thought I wasn't looking, I heard you say a prayer, and I believed there is a God I could always talk to.

When you thought I wasn't looking, I felt you kiss me good night, and I felt loved.

When you thought I wasn't looking, I saw tears come from your eyes, and I learned that sometimes things hurt, but it's all right to cry.

When you thought I wasn't looking, I saw that you cared and I wanted to be everything that I could be.

When you thought I wasn't looking, I looked...and wanted to say thanks for all the things I saw when you thought I wasn't looking.

- Author Unknown

Treat Them Better Than They Are

A teenager was brought before a judge to be sentenced for a crime. The judge saw many good qualities in the boy and talked to him privately. "Tell me, son, why did you do it?" The boy replied, "I guess I just lived up to what people expected of me."

It is one of the great facts of life that people become what we expect them to be. Goethe said once, "Treat a person as he is and he remains as he is, but treat him better than he is and he will become better."

Experiments have shown that when people treat young persons as if they were senile, they actually develop symptoms of senility.

Some years ago a man who was on trial for his life said, "My father always said I was no good. Mother said I would never amount to anything. The school teacher said I was worthless. Even my home town people said I would become a criminal. And I always wondered why. I was just like the other boys, only a bit more independent. The only creature that ever seemed to believe in me was my dog. My dog died and I became an outcast."

They Live Up to Our Expectations

Give a boy a bad name, and he'll live up to it.

On the other hand, when a person shows sincere interest in us, when we know that someone has great faith and confidence in us, something within us responds. We respect ourselves more; we try to measure up to the confidence and trust placed in us. This is what being loved means. When someone loves us, it is as if he held a crown over our heads which henceforth we must try to grow tall enough to wear. "I love you," wrote Elizabeth Ferguson von Hesse, "not only for what you are but for what I am when I am with you. I love you not only for what you have made of yourself but what you are making of me . . . I love you for ignoring the possibilities of the fool in me and laying firm hold of the possibilities of good in me."

It is hard to beat J.B. Priestly's understanding of feminine psychology: "She was not pretty, but she might have been handsome if somebody had kept telling her that she was pretty."

Dorothy Sarnoff, originator of Speech Dynamics, says that at the age of seven she considered herself the ugliest child in the neighborhood. She was painfully shy. Fortunately a teacher was able to help her. "She kept telling me that I could do things. And because she told me I could, I did."

Treat a person better than he is and he will become better. We treat our dogs as if they were "almost human": that is why they become almost human. A mother teaches her baby to talk by talking to it as if it understood long before it really does. This is why the higher thing always raises the lower.

A class of fourth graders was given to a teacher who was told that all the children in the class were of superior intelligence. Actually they were all of very average intelligence. But the teacher worked with them on the basis that they were of superior intelligence. The result was that the intelligence of the class increased phenomenally.

Writing to the Christians in Corinth, St. Paul shows what great confidence he has in them. "I have great confidence in you; I have great pride in you; I am filled with comfort" (2

Cor. 7:4). "I rejoice because I have perfect confidence in you" (2 Cor. 7:16). He was challenging them to live up to the confidence he had in them.

Praise, when sincerely given, has an almost magical power to transform. If you would like to see a person progress toward full maturity, congratulate him on his accomplishments, but do it sincerely.

"Treat a person as he is and he remains as he is, but treat him as if he were better than he is, and he will become better."

The Approach of Jesus

This is the approach Jesus used with Judas. The Master was well aware that there was a traitor within the ranks. But he tried to show Judas that He had confidence in him. He did not treat him like a traitor but like a friend. He even made him treasurer of the group. It was as if He were saying to him, "Judas, I need you. I want you to serve as treasurer. I have confidence in you." The appeal failed with Judas, but the fact remains that the best way to reclaim someone who is on the wrong way is not to treat him with suspicion but with trust, not as if we expect the worst from him but the best.

Where do our impressions about ourselves come from? Primarily from our parents and parental figures. The way they treat us when we are children makes us form strong opinions about what we are and what we can expect from ourselves. These opinions are strongest in our subconscious mind, down inside where you can't see them too clearly most of the time.

If parents treat us as though we're O.K., we believe we're O.K. If they treat us as though we're uncontrollable, we take it for granted that we are uncontrollable, by anyone, even ourselves. Most of the people who go overboard with uncontrollable habits like smoking, alcoholism, drug addiction are those who subconsciously think they're uncontrollable and have to reinforce that idea-because whatever you think about yourself, whether it's something good or bad, you automatically do everything you can to prove it so.

How important to treat our children as though they are better than they are in order to keep discouraging the bad and reinforcing the good in them.

The Way God Treats Us

We have talked about how important it is that we treat people, especially our children, as if they were better than they are, in order to challenge them to become better. But we have not yet spoken the most important part of this truth, i.e., this is exactly how God treats us. He looks at sinners and sees potential saints. He looks at Saul the persecutor and sees Paul the apostle. He looks at Simon the unstable fisherman and sees Peter the rock. He looks at Zacchaeus the dishonest tax collector and sees Zacchaeus the compassionate philanthropist. "While we were yet sinners God sent His Son to die for us." God believes in us. He believes in us so much that He sent His Son to die for us. He gave us commandments and challenges of staggering height because He believed that people through His grace and power could rise to become "partakers of divine nature" (St. Peter). When God accepts and receives the sinner back again, He treats him not as a criminal but as an honored guest. Witness how the father welcomed back the prodigal son. He did not treat him as if he could never trust him again; he welcomed him as a son and declared a feast to celebrate his return.

Examples

We are to treat others as God treats us.

I heard a priest who works with boys say once that delinquent boys behaved like black sheep because everyone expected them to be black sheep. He himself treated them as white sheep and most of them-he said-became white sheep.

Floyd Starr used to run a school for boys who had been in trouble with the law. He was convinced that there was no such thing as a "bad" boy. If a boy behaved badly, he said, it was because he had been treated badly, somewhere along the line, by life, or by his parents, or by something.

Floyd told once of driving into town with one of his boys who was sullen, withdrawn, difficult to reach. When they got to their destination, Floyd took ten dollars from his pocket and handed it to the youngster. "I'll be busy for an hour or so," he said. "Get yourself some lunch and bring me the change. And here are the keys to the car, in case you need it."

The boy looked at him unbelieving. "Have you forgotten what I was arrested for, Mr. Starr? It was car stealing."

"I know," said Starr. "But that's all behind you now. I believe in you. I trust you."

The boy's eyes filled with tears, "Oh," he said brokenly, "Why didn't my father or mother ever say that?"

Parental Tugs

A commanding officer stood at rigid attention at an airfield where he was stationed. He had trained a group of young men in the art of flying. Now one of them was climbing into his plane for his first solo flight. The officer was tense as the boy taxied the plane out to the runway. When the signal came from the tower, the plane sped down the runway, climbed into the air, and flew smoothly into the far horizon. Then for the first time the commanding officer relaxed as he smiled and said, "Well, he's on his own now."

How quickly our children grow! How quickly the day comes when they must leave our lives-for college, for work, for marriage, for other things that take them away-beyond where we can follow, beyond where we can go. Now they are on their own. Now they must fly solo. Now they must go their own way; they must choose their own friends; they must make their own decisions. We can rejoice with them; we can weep over them; but we can no longer accompany them or decide for them.

Preparing Them for Independence

We complain that children are too independent. The tragedy is not independence; the tragedy lies in the simple fact that we have not prepared them for independence. We have thrown them into the world, unprepared for the turmoil and the tumult and the contentions and the temptations that they have to face. We have not prepared them for the time when they must fly solo. The trouble is not with their independence; the trouble is with their unpreparedness, and that is to be charged clearly to the thoughtlessness and to the self-indulgence of parents.

What are we doing today as parents-what can we do-to prepare our children for independence?

The first thing we can do is to understand the tremendous importance of the early years in a child's life. It is in the first ten years of a child's life that we can plant a sense of values, not only by what we teach about God, but also by the way we live. A child's little brain is like a recording instrument, and what it records can never be erased. If, in building a wall, the bricks at the bottom, near the foundation, are crooked, then no matter how straight the bricks are on top, the wall will be crooked. So it is with childhood experiences. They constitute the foundation of life. If the foundation is straight and secure, so will be the wall.

Two eminent psychologists (Peck and Havighurst) write:

"The general conclusion seems inescapable that a child's character is the direct product, almost a direct reproduction, of the way his parents treat him. As they are to him, so he is to all others."

If they love him, he will love others. If they hate him, he will hate. If they treat him with respect, he will respect himself and others.

From one's table manners to his manner of looking at life, from his honor to his health, his swearing to his praying, his truthfulness to his trustworthiness, the home will get its way. What happens to him later in life, from the crime he commits to the emotional illness to which he falls heir, can be traced directly or indirectly to those indelible years when he was in the palm of the hands of parents.

Who Teaches Religion?

Religion is not learned in church or Sunday school where a child spends only 1% of his time, but at home where the child spends 83% of his time. A famous Greek Orthodox archbishop said once that he did not learn religion at seminary. He learned religion at home by watching his mother pray every day before the family icon. How many of us sit back and expect the church to teach our children religion? The church and Sunday school do not teach religion; they are merely reinforcers of what the child learns at home.

Every child needs a powerful guide, a living example, someone to follow, someone to pattern after, someone to set standards, someone in whose footsteps he would wish to walk! Where will he find this pattern, this standard, this example? Will he find it in his parents at home? Or will he find it on the street? In the gutter? In some bull session? On the movie screen? Or somewhere else?

A young mother was shocked to hear her little boy tell a lie. She took the lad on her knee and explained how bad it is to lie. "Now, you won't tell a lie again, will you?" she asked him. "No, Mom," replied the lad, "you can tell 'em better than I can."

Worthy of Our Respect

We want to be proud of our children. Is it possible that they want to be proud of us? We want our children to honor us? Are we giving them something worth honoring? We want our children to respect us? Are we offering them an example worthy of respect?

It is true that times have changed. But they do not

always change for the better. One suburban mother recently said, "My home has turned into a filling station. My two sons and daughter just come in at meal times to get filled up. Then out they go." But it was not always like this. Not so long ago the family was well nigh everything. It was a school, for it was in the family that we first found the books which molded our judgments. The family was the church; for it was in our homes most of us heard our first prayers. There we saw father and mother praying before the family icon. The family was not a filling station. It was a home-a God centered home. It is this kind of home which, St. Chrysostom says, produces champions for Christ!

Respect Each Child

Finally, we, as parents, must not only expect our children to honor us, but we should also honor and respect them. Children deserve respect because they are persons. They may be little, they are frequently immature, but they are growing persons. And the only way that they can grow into maturity is if we, their parents, allow and encourage them to grow. We must treat them not as objects but as persons. When we exercise parental discipline, we must exercise it for the good of the children-not for the good of the parents.

When Jesus was 12 years old, He had accompanied his parents to Jerusalem; but instead of leaving Jerusalem with them, He had stayed behind in the Temple, talking with theologians. Naturally, His mother, not realizing that He could have any other duty apart from pleasing her and avoiding trouble to her, reprimanded Him sharply when she found Him again. But Jesus replied firmly: "How is it that you sought Me? Did you not know that I must be in my Father's house?" At twelve years of age Jesus is in the process of detaching Himself from His mother, of becoming Himself, discovering His own vocation; He is not destined to be what His mother imagines, but what God is calling Him to be. And we, as parents and elders, must ever respect the God-given individuality of our children and help them grow up to be not what we want them to be but what God has equipped them to be.

Have you ever seen tiny tugboats pushing a giant ocean liner from its berth on the dock out through the harbor to the ocean? Are not we parents like these tugboats when we direct the growth of our children? Always working together, we give a little push here, a little pull there-parental tugs! In this way, with God's guidance, we steer our children to the ocean of life. Once there, we pray and trust that they are prepared to launch out of the harbor of the home on their own true course!

A mother said once of her young son: "I realize I can't go with him everywhere, so I am building him up from within."

Henri Nouwen wrote, "Our children are our most important guests, who enter into our homes, ask for careful attention, stay for a while, and then leave to follow their own way."

Are You Listening?

"Dad's not the type who sits and listens. He sits and tells you how it is." "We rarely discuss anything important at home. We used to talk at dinner, but now that's out. Dad bought a portable TV and put it in the dining room." "I can't ask my mother any questions about sex, because right away she fires back, 'What do you want to know for?'"

If we adults wish to do something constructive for young people today, the best *place* to begin is in our homes. The best *way* to begin is by encouraging young people to talk freely about the problems that confront them. We must learn to listen as well as give pontifical advice and commands.

If we expect young people to listen to us perhaps we can show them how by listening to them.

Seventy years ago one of the most important events in the world of psychology took place. A doctor did something new. He treated an intelligent young girl suffering from a hysterical disorder by simply listening to her for hundreds of hours. She talked herself out, finally, and Dr. Sigmund Freud had discovered the great therapeutic value of listening which today has become one of the basic techniques of psychiatry.

Hear the Unspoken Cries

Good listening requires that we be sensitive to the needs of others. We cannot be sensitive unless we have anchored our lives in the love of Christ. How sensitive were the ears of Jesus! He could hear the unspoken cries of people in need. His sympathy was so quick and His hearing so acute that He was aware of human need when others around Him heard nothing.

Imagine a mother sleeping with a baby in her arms. The clock ticks loudly, but she sleeps on. The buses rattle past the window, but she sleeps on. Doors bang, kitchen noises ascend, milkmen shout, dogs bark; she sleeps on. But let the baby stir a foot or an arm, let it but move in its sleep, let it but utter the echo of a cry, and *at once* the mother is wide awake. What is it that makes a mother so sensitive to the cries of her child? What else but love.

A Christian who is possessed of the love of Christ is sensitive. He is tuned in to his fellow humans so that he can hear meaningful overtones in many conversations. He is sensitive to the cries for help, for understanding, for acceptance, for love, and he responds accordingly.

Let's look at an example. One high-school youngster arriving home on Saturday night at one o'clock, came into the bedroom of his parents and said, "Mom and Dad, I want to talk to you. I don't want any advice. Just listen." He talked for an hour and a half about school, about his moral concerns, his friends and their parents, and about his religious beliefs. His mother and father said nothing. They just listened. Then quite suddenly the boy got up. "Thanks for listening," he said. "I probably won't talk to you like this again for a year." With that he went to bed.

Imagine the damage those parents would have caused if they had not been sensitive to the needs of their son and had said, "Look here, it's one o'clock in the morning. Can't you see we're half asleep. How dare you barge in here and disturb our sleep. Talk to us about it tomorrow when we're awake."

Listen with Your Eyes

A little girl danced into the kitchen where her mother was busy preparing dinner. "Mother," she said, "guess what!"

"I don't know-what?" the mother asked, not looking up from the potato she was peeling.

"Mother, you're not listening."

"Yes I am, honey." She pushed the peelings into the garbage disposal.

"But, mother, you're not listening with your eyes."

Listening is hard work. It takes all of oneself not just the ears but the eyes, the mind, the heart, the whole person. We listen not only to what the vocal cords tell us but also to what the whole body of the other person is saying.

"Remember When I Was Seven . . . ."

Let me share with you a part of a letter that moved me deeply. It was written by a boy with a record as a juvenile delinquent. He wrote it to his parents, who sent it to a Kansas City newspaper with a note reading: "Perhaps, if we share this letter through your newspaper, it will help other parents."

"Dear Folks,

"Thank you for everything, but I am going to Chicago and try and start some kind of new life.

"You asked me why I did those things and why I gave you so much trouble, and the answer is easy for me to give you, but I am wondering if you will understand.

"Remember when I was about six or seven and I used to want you just to listen to me? I remember all the nice things you gave me for Christmas and my birthday and I was really happy with the things-about a week-but the rest of the time I just wanted . . . you to listen to me. But you said you were busy.

"Mom, you are a wonderful cook, and you had everything so clean and you were tired so much from doing all things that made you busy; but you know something, Mom? I would have liked crackers and peanut butter as well-if you had only sat down with me a while during the day and said to me, 'Tell me all about it so I can maybe help you understand' . . . .

"I think that all the kids who are doing so many things that grown-ups are tearing out their hair worrying about are really looking for somebody who will have the time to listen for a few minutes. . . .

"If anybody asks you where I am, tell them I've gone looking for somebody with time because I've got a lot of things I want to talk about.

Love to all,

Your Son."

Everybody's Doing It

The other day I heard someone say, "Don't you think that very often when people get involved in drugs or alcoholism or sex it's because they're just following the crowd, adopting the lower group standards around them instead of sticking to their own higher standards, the standards of Christ?" There is no doubt that there are real pressures that push people into this kind of conformity. A ninth-grade Sunday school teacher said:

"My ninth grade Sunday school class was having a lesson on 'conformity' and we were talking about how necessary young people find it not to be too 'different.' If galoshes are 'out' (which they usually are in winter), then any teenager would rather arrive at school soaked to the waist and with icicles hanging from his knee-caps than appear in a pair of boots!

"My ninth graders cheerfully admitted all this. But they were rather taken aback when I asked, 'Well, then, if one of you girls is walking down the hall in school in a new dress and you are suddenly confronted with another girl wearing the exact same dress as yours, why do you go into a tizzy?'

"The girls giggled guiltily and the boys smirked.

"Then one girl said, 'Well, we don't want to be exactly like someone else!'

"Another added, 'I guess we want to be the same-but different!'"

It isn't only teen-agers who "want to be the same-but different." All of us want this, because we need to feel a sense of security. One of the ways we get it is by conforming, by being like the rest, to feel that we're part of the human race. But, if, like the two girls wearing the same dress, we find ourselves being *too much the same* as everyone else, we don't like it. We get bored. We feel insulted. We look for something new.

Why is this so?

We Are Originals Not Copies

God made each of us different. Of all the billions of people in the world, no two have the same fingerprints, or the same personality, or DNA. But instead of rejoicing in this individuality, very often we decide we must be like everyone else in the group. We take this divine gift of uniqueness and water it down until it disappears. As someone so well said, "Most people are born originals but they end up as copies."

This is really a form of immorality, because when we begin to reject our specialness, it's like telling God that we don't want to be the special person He created us to be. We also begin to lose our freedom. The person who goes along with the group is not a free person. He's really not living his own life; he's letting others live it for him. He has to follow the herd, and he has little or nothing to say about where the herd is going. He begins to lose the capacity to think and act for himself. Finally he gets to the point where he hopes someone else will tell him what to do or where to go. The result is that he is no longer a unique person created in the image of God but a mere statistic.

A Demonic Ploy

There is something demonic about this. We know that the devil always tries to remain anonymous. If he appeared as the devil, no one would follow him. So he takes on many disguises. St. Paul says that he appears as "an angel of light." One of the devil's favorite tactics is to make you believe that "everybody's doing it," that it's the spirit of the times. And, if you're not doing it, you must be queer, not "up with it" and behind the times. The tempter will never say, "Come, I'll teach you a sin." He will always say, "Look, let me show you something interesting, something pleasurable, something that will enrich your life and make you really popular."

The Worship of Public Opinion

In so doing, the tempter works on one of our weaknesses, namely, the worship of public opinion. A century ago Harriet Martineau wrote that the worship of public opinion was the established religion of America. Since then, we have established the American Institute of Public Opinion, the Gallup Poll and countless other polls and agencies to taste public opinion on every conceivable matter.

In our secular world, trends and tendencies are more important than principles and morals. After all, we've heard it said over and over, "Fifty million Frenchmen can't be wrong." Well, fifty-million *opinions* may make an idea *popular* but they don't make it right. Fifty-million wrong ideas don't add up to wisdom. They merely add up to a colossal error. If one man's opinion is wrong to begin with, it doesn't become right just because it becomes popular. Truth is no respecter of numbers. It was the majority of public opinion that condemned Jesus to death. "What shall I do with him?" Pilate asked the crowd. And the crowd (public opinion) replied, "Crucify him! Crucify him!"

It's a good thing Columbus did not worship the public opinion of his time that the world was flat, or the Wright brothers that man could never fly!

The worship of this false god of public opinion has even reached into some churches. One theologian was heard saying, "The moral code that we've been teaching has to be changed. Not two percent of our people believe in it or live by it anymore, and what good is a moral code if no one lives up to it?"

This pseudo-theologian should read the word of God a little more than he does the Gallup Poll, especially Matthew 5:18 where Jesus said, "For truly I say to you, till heaven and earth pass away, not an iota, not a dot, will pass from the law until all is accomplished." Our authority for right and wrong rests not on the number of people who accept it, but on God who has revealed it. His law does not change to accommodate the frailties of human nature.

"When in Rome"

Another tactic used to try to get us to follow the crowd is the advice contained in the well-known words, "When in Rome, do as the Romans do." When people tell us this, we should ask them, "Which Romans? the poor? the middle class? the rich? the clergy? the man who sells bananas? the Communists? the Pope?" You see, they're all living in Rome. And they're not doing the same thing. How can I possibly know what they're all doing? And why should I follow them? Why shouldn't I be original? Why shouldn't I do my own "thing'? Why not follow my own principles?

Other tactics are used to try to get us to follow the crowd. For example, we should realize that a person who is living in sin feels very insecure, anxious and guilty about it. These feelings unconsciously impel him to pull as many other people as possible into the same boat with him. The more companions in guilt he has, the lighter his burden of individual guilt feels. The person who can look around his little world and say, "Everybody's doing it; I'm no different," momentarily feels less guilty and anxious. So we must beware of these people trying to drag us down to the gutter with them to help alleviate their guilt feelings.

St. Anthony said once, "A time is coming when men will go mad, and when they see someone who is not mad, they will attack him saying, 'You are mad, you are not like us.'"

Salt and Light

The Christian is *in* the world but not *of* the world. Where the world goes opposite to Christ, the Christian opposes the world. He swims not with the current but against it. He doesn't behave as the world behaves. He is different. "You are the salt of the earth," said Jesus. "You are the light of the world."

It reminds one of the Gulf Stream. As it winds its way north in the Atlantic, the water around it gets colder and colder. Yet no matter how cold the water around it, the water in the Gulf Stream itself remains warm. It is never chilled by the surrounding water. It maintains its own mild temperature in the midst of water that gets bitterly cold. This is a picture of the true Christian. He does not take on the temperature of the world around him. He is a thermostat instead of a thermometer. Instead of being affected by the climate, he creates the climate.

Why Is the Christian Different?

The Christian is different because he is "in Christ." St. Paul uses this phrase more than eighty times in his letters. The Christian never forgets the presence of Christ; he walks with Christ every day; the blood of Jesus flows in his very veins; he makes no decision without asking the guidance of Christ; he attempts no task without the help of Christ. He is in Christ just as really as he is in the air he breathes. This is why St. Peter called the early Christians a radically different people: "You are a chosen race, a royal priesthood, a holy nation, God's own people, that you may declare the wonderful deeds of him who called you out of darkness into his marvelous light" (I Peter 2:9).

Orthodox Christian parents have to "stick to their guns." By that we mean expressing what they believe as best they can, setting standards and guidelines and sticking by them. We are learning that our children are grateful for the standards and the rules on which we insisted in the past. This was very difficult at the time because of their resistance due to peer pressure ("Everybody's doing it.") Perhaps Christian parents should get together and insist on a little peer pressure of their own.

The Power of Encouragement / Affirmation

What children need most is encouragement: the encouragement of God, which we have; the encouragement of the Scriptures, which we have; and the encouragement of God's people, especially parents toward their children, which we do not always have. And which we so desperately need. One person shared that when he was a child, his mother would whisper in his ear as she tucked him into bed. "You're such a special child, I think God must have sent you to do something special. I hope you find out what it is." He said, "I didn't know until years later that she was whispering the same thing to my sister and little brother." Isn't this the way Jesus treated people-people like Zacchaeus, the Samaritan woman, Peter who denied him three times, and so many others? Through His forgiveness Jesus encouraged people to grow and achieve their full potential as children of God. This is how Zacchaeus the dishonest tax collector went on to become Zacchaeus the benevolent philanthropist; this is how the adulterous Samaritan woman who had five so-called "husbands" became St. Photini, one of the first evangelists; and this is how the weak, vacillating Peter became Peter the Rock, the chief of the apostles. The encouragement sinners received through Christ's forgiveness made them new persons.

One of the good points of modern psychology is the emphasis that is placed on affirmation. We all have a deep need to be affirmed, encouraged, and praised. Psychologists have recognized that there is so much tearing down going on in our culture that people are destroying one another with words. One psychologist discovered that the average child receives 431 negative messages on an average day: "Your shirt is filthy . . . Your closet is a mess . . . Your hair is too long . . . Get off the phone-now! etc." One parent prayed at the end of the day, "Another day gone by and not once did I say, 'I love you. Dear Lord, forgive me.'"

Criticism keeps telling people they are no good. Yet what people need most is not criticism but encouragement. People have a way of becoming what they are encouraged to be, not what they are nagged to be. How often we try to transmit values by criticism, "Why is your room so messy?" "Why are you so careless about money?" Yet how often do we praise our children when their rooms are neat or when they have handled money well? Values are transmitted far more effectively through praise than through criticism, fear and guilt. One father said that once when his daughter was 11 years old, he asked her, "Cathy, do you know that I love you?" She answered, "I've always sort of thought you did, but you've never told me." How long will Cathy have to wait?

If a Child Lives with . . .

If a child lives with criticism, she learns to condemn.
If a child lives with hostility, he learns to fight.
If a child lives with fears, she learns to be apprehensive.
If a child lives with jealousy, she learns to feel guilty.
If a child lives with encouragement, he learns to be confident.
If a child lives with tolerance, she learns to be patient.
If a child lives with praise, he learns to be apprecia-

tive.

If a child lives with acceptance, she learns to love.

If a child lives with approval, he learns to like himself.

If a child lives with fairness, he learns what justice is.

If a child lives with honesty, she learns what truth is.

If a child lives with security, he learns to have faith in himself and in those about him.

If a child lives with friendliness, she learns that the world is a good place in which to live.

Anonymous

"It Takes A Village to Raise a Child"- Which Village?

It is often said that "it takes a village to raise a child." The village is indeed important, but we must never abdicate the responsibility of raising a child solely to the "village." Christian parents are personally responsible for nurturing their child's body, mind and spirit. If they are not doing so, it is the responsibility of the "village" i.e., the church, to remind them and assist them of this moral and spiritual obligation. St. Paul tells us in Eph. 4:15-16 about the peculiar Christian "village" which is the Church. What do we mean by the world "village"? Do we mean schools where prayer is not allowed and God's name may not be mentioned? Is this the "village" that you think should raise your child? Do we mean degrading TV shows and movies, that introduce the gutter experiences of life into the minds and hearts of our children? Is this the "village" that you would want to raise your children? It seems that today we need to protect our children from that kind of "village"! It takes a Christian mother and father who know the Lord and truly love their children and are willing to spend time with them sharing God's values. The true "village" for the Orthodox Christian is not the secular world but the family and the church!

Mother's Role Before Birth

Scientists have known for years that before children are born they are influenced by the mother's behavior. For example, the link between the mother's smoking and low birth weight is firmly established as is the use of alcohol during pregnancy with neurological damage to the unborn child. The mother, even before giving birth, does not only give shape to the child's body, but also, in an indirect way, to the child's whole personality. Therefore, it makes sense that: "religious instruction should begin in the womb." The mother's love of God, her love for her baby, her love for her family are all communicated to the child in the womb. If the mother thinks of her child as a gift from God, that child will be a gift, but if she thinks of her child as being unwanted then the child will feel unwanted and respond accordingly. If the mother is under undue stress from her family, the child will perceive this stress, but if the family is supportive, the child's personality will be influenced by that support and the feeling of well-being that comes with it. When the mother receives the Eucharist, I believe the child shares somehow in the grace of the Real Presence of Jesus Christ in the Holy Eucharist. The Orthodox Church has always believed that life begins at conception.

Internalizing the Faith Through Love

Studies have shown that children learn from those they love. If they love you, children will eagerly accept your faith and your value system. If they do not love you, they will rebel. Hence, the importance of creating a family atmosphere where love prevails. This cannot be done without God and family prayer, without carving out time to be completely present to God and to each other. Someone said, "Whom you would change, you must first love." A child comes to know God's love through the love he experiences from his parents.

The first icon of God a child ever sees is the icon of mother or father leaning over the crib. The love of parents is not just an analogy for the love of God; it reveals God's love. The child learns to love by first being loved in the home. Children can love because they were first loved (I John 4:10; 4:19). And for this, the role of the parents is central. Thus, the most important thing in a family is LOVE, that the parents love each other. Only thus, can they create an atmosphere at home where love prevails. "Now abide faith, hope and love. The greatest of these is love."

Bruno Bettelheim, the famous child psychologist, said that a child's moral choices are not based on abstract choices of right and wrong. They are based on the people he loves and admires. In Bettelheim's words, "The question for the child is not, 'Do I want to be good?' but 'Whom do I love and want to be like?'" When Augustine, for example, wrote about the person who was most instrumental in converting him to Christianity, Bishop Ambrose of Milan, he said, "That man of God received me as a father and showed me kindness. I began to love him, at first not as a teacher of truth, but as a person who was kind to me." Who can estimate the value of a parent who radiates the love and kindness of Christ to his/her children? In the words of Mother Teresa, "Be the living expression of God's kindness; kindness in your face, kindness in your eyes, kindness in your smile, kindness in your warm greeting . . . Spread love everywhere. First of all in your own house." Our children will not be *argued* into faith by logical arguments. They will be *loved* into faith, just as the prodigal son was not *argued* but *loved* back to the Father.

Prayer Projects for the Home

Two hectic places in most households are the bathroom and the kitchen. We all at least glance in the bathroom mirror in the morning, and open the refrigerator door a couple of times a day. Both of these "homey" objects offer opportunities to fit prayer into our daily routines. If everybody in the household would compose or find a short prayer each week and put it on the bathroom mirror or refrigerator next to a paper icon, perhaps everyone would read them. There are many ways to bring variety and to make prayer more meaningful, especially in the family setting.

In church, the priest has a diptych at the altar, a little booklet containing the names of people he is to pray for. Why not do the same at home? Make a diptych, a Prayer Concern Folder of construction paper. Label it Our Family Prayer Concerns. Adults and children alike are better able to visualize concerns and be specific in praying if pictures are used for each prayerful concern. Gather photographs of persons you wish to pray for-parents, grandparents, friends. Cut pictures that represent specific concerns-hunger, war, missionaries-from magazines or newspapers. At mealtime, each person chooses the picture he/she will pray for. After all have prayed, return the pictures to the folder to be used at the next prayer time.

The Gift of Your Presence

O. Henry, the American master of the short story, has a story in which he tells of a little girl whose mother was dead. Her father used to come home from work and sit down and take off his jacket and open his paper and light his pipe and put his feet on the ottoman. The little girl would come in and would ask him to play with her for a little for she was lonely. He told her he was tired, to let him be at peace. He told her to go out to the street and play. She played on the streets. The inevitable happened-she took to the streets. The years passed on and she died. Then O. Henry's vision extended to heaven. The girl's soul arrived at the pearly gates. Peter saw her and said to Jesus, "Master, here's a girl who was a bad lot. I suppose we send her straight to hell?" "No," said Jesus gently, "let her in." And then His eyes grew stern. "But look for a man who refused to play with his little girl and who sent her out to the streets and SEND HIM TO HELL."

How many expensive gifts that parents give their children, and husbands give their wives at Christmas are given to atone for the guilt they feel for spending so little time with them. We attempt to offer in expensive gifts what we have not offered in the eloquence of loving deeds and words. And yet the best gift a parent can give his child, and a husband his wife, is the gift of their time, their presence; nothing can ever make up for this.

Parents who set time aside to spend with their children are saying to the children, "We love you. You are important to us." One woman reminisced once about an important experience in her childhood. It was a particular vacation her family took together. She said, "My favorite remembrance is a trip we took to Washington, D.C., when I was twelve. I'll never forget my father pointing out all the monuments to us. I was proud that he was giving us so much of his attention. I felt important and grown up. I felt loved."

Leave Them A Legacy of Happy Memories

"Tread softly-the years roll out a carpet of memories for our hearts to walk on."

What we do today as parents with our children creates memories that will bless or break them tomorrow.

"The moment may be temporary," someone said, "but the memory is forever."

"Remembrance is the only paradise out of which you cannot be driven for if you don't have memories, you can't have dreams" (Liz Erickson).

How important it is that we build up a storehouse of worthwhile memories for our children when they are young.

We read in that classic of Orthodox spirituality, *Treasury of Russian Spirituality*:

"Why are childhood impressions so important? Why is it essential to fill a child's mind and soul with knowledge and good example, beginning with the very earliest states of its life? In children we find undiminished the capacity for faith, simplicity, gentleness, pliability, compassion, imagination and meekness. Now this is precisely the soil which yields a harvest many thousand times greater than the seed which has been sown. When, later in life, the soul has become as hard as flint, a man can be purified, saved, by the residues of his childhood experience. This is why it is so important to keep children close to the church-it will give them food for their entire lifetime."

A former prisoner of war tells how he was thrown into solitary confinement by Hitler. Everything he had was taken from him. The only thing he had left was his memory. It proved to be his salvation. He found strength and sanity by repeating to himself over and over again the psalms, the hymns, and the Bible verses he had memorized at home as a boy. He was saved by his childhood memories.

A college football player came to his friend one day and confided that he had made a mess of his life. "I am going to come back and start over again," he said. "Do you know what has kept me from going to pieces? It was the memory of my father's prayers. You don't know what it means to a boy to have heard his father pray, especially when his father lives out his prayers."

He was saved by his childhood memories.

One father makes it a practice to take each child out to lunch separately at least once each month. Often it's just for a hamburger. But the parent devotes himself completely to the one child and his or her own special needs. The child feels specially and personally loved. How can this not leave the child with a legacy of unforgettable memories?

One of the purposes for the family practices suggested in this book is to help Orthodox Christian families create memories that will inspire their children for their entire lifetime.

A young mother adopted a philosophy that whenever there was a conflict between her house and her children, her children would always get her attention. She reasoned, "No one will remember or care 10 or 15 years from now that the living room carpet was not clean on a certain day. But 10 or 15 years from now it will matter a lot whether or not I had time for my children on that day or any other day. They will remember."

What will your children say about you 15 years from now? What will their fondest memories be? What are you doing today to make such memories possible?

A family in Colorado tried for years to save enough

money to replace their ancient bathroom fixtures. But each year as skiing time rolled around, the bathroom money went for a family ski trip. The parents are happy it turned out this way. The children are now grown and married, but when they write home to the parents they talk about the good times they had skiing together. Reminiscing, the father said, "I can't imagine my son writing and saying, 'Dad, I sure remember our swell bathroom.'"

Take time to cultivate happy memories.

God Loves Us Even When We Are Bad

God loves us just as we are. (Not necessarily as we do.) He pursues us with His love. Believing this helps us to understand the love husband and wife should have for each other and for their children. It is love with no strings attached; we don't have to prove ourselves to God; we don't earn His love. Understanding this is fundamental to all relationships between husband and wife, parents and children.

It follows from this that we must accept everyone within the family, trust our children and love them just as they are. (But again, not necessary for what they do.) For example, how many of our children have reason to wonder about our love for them on the basis of our reaction to their report cards or whether they make the team.

A social worker told the story of Johnny-an incurably bad boy who lived in an orphanage. Many couples had taken him home with the thought of adopting him, but each time they returned him to the orphanage.

One day a young couple visited the orphanage, saw Johnny and asked about him. They were told of his bad record. A few days later they called to say that they would like to adopt him. When asked if they would like to take him on trial for a few weeks, they refused. They insisted on adopting him as he was.

Johnny went home with them, and it wasn't long before he got into trouble again. He blurted out, "Aren't you going to send me back? All the others did."

"No, Johnny, we're not going to send you back. We want you to be with us."

"You mean you will keep me, even if I'm bad?"

"Yes," they replied. "We adopted you as our son. You will always be our son. And we will love you as our son. The only way that you will ever go away now is if you leave us. But we will never leave you. When you're bad we love you with a love that is sad. When you're good, we love you with a love that is happy. but we will always love you."

This love that accepted Johnny as he was, changed his life.*

The is exactly the way God loves us. It is simply not true to say that God loves us only if we are good. He loves us always. It is this love that parents are called upon to reflect to each other and to their children.

Ask yourself: Do I love my children unconditionally, or on a brownie-point system?

---

* I am indebted for this story to Orin D. Thompson's book "Even If I'm Bad." Augsburg Publishing House.

On Being Completly Present

Mark Van Doren said once:

"There is one thing we can do, and the happiest people are those who do it to the limit of their ability.

"We can be completely present. We can be all there. We can control the tendency of our minds to wander from the situation we are in toward yesterday, toward tomorrow, toward something we have forgotten, toward some other place we are going next. It is hard to do this, but it is harder to understand afterward wherein it was we fell so short. It was where and when we ceased to give our entire attention to the person, the opportunity, before us.

"Those who have fewest regrets are those who take each moment as it comes for all that it is worth. It will never come again, for worse or better. It is ours alone; we can make it what we will."

Eating We Do Not Eat

A story that has come out of Zen literature concerns a master's conversation with a monk:

"Do you ever make an effort to get disciplined in the truth?"

"Yes, I do."

"How do you exercise yourself?"

"When I am hungry, I eat; when I am tired, I sleep."

"This is what everybody does; can they be said to be exercising themselves in the same way you do?"

"No."

"Why not?"

"Because when they eat, they do not eat, but are thinking

on various other things, thereby allowing themselves to be disturbed; when they sleep they do not sleep, but dream of a thousand and one things which interfere with their sleep. This is why they are not like me."

How seldom it is that we are completely present to what we are doing at the moment. Take the following example:

The middle-aged businessman seated at the family dinner table is concerned about his need for an operation, about the expenses involved, about the deadlines he must meet before he can take time off from his work, about the possible complications following surgery. These concerns pass through his mind to the extent that he is barely conscious of his food or of his loved ones sitting at the table with him.

His son, eating at the same table, might be thinking about the girl he met between classes. Preoccupied with her, he is completely oblivious of his father and his mother eating with him.

His mother, sitting next to him at the table, might be worrying about something else that keeps her attention from the family dinner and causes her great anxiety.

None of these persons, although they are members of the same family and sitting at the same table, is completely present to each other. They are miles away from each other, wrapped up in their own thoughts and fears about tomorrow. Not being really present, they are complete strangers to each other.

One of the worst things we can do to our children is to give them half of our interest, because to give them half of our interest is to give them half of ourselves. A half-wit is someone who is only half there.

The Greatest Kind of Love

Suppose you came to me, a priest, at church and I kept glancing at my watch, worrying about my next appointment. You would be deeply hurt by this, because I would not be giving you my full attention. You would be less open than if you had my complete attention that moment. *You* experienced by nervousness, my being in a hurry, my lack of attentiveness as a lack of interest in *you*. And this turns you off completely. So, almost automatically, by being completely present to people, by behaving as if the person who is with us at the moment is the only person who exists, by giving them our total undivided attention when we are with them, a relationship can become more real, more loving, and more life-changing.

Being completely present to people may be the greatest kind of love we can give them. For in a strange way, we are giving them our whole attention. Perhaps this is the most real way to value a person as a human being-to really be *with* him and take him seriously as he is. A single such contact may change the whole direction of a life.

A young woman told of an experience she had when she was twelve years old. Dr. Elton Trueblood, the great Christian philosopher and preacher, was speaking in the city in which she lived. He was staying in her parents' home. She related that during the few days he was there, he talked to her, asking her questions, and really listened to what she had to say, just as he did to her parents. She said that although he never knew it, that brief experience as a Christian girl of being taken as an authentic, intelligent Christian had made her want deeply to be one, and had changed the direction of her life.

The Example of Jesus

A truly great example of this is our Lord Jesus Christ who was always completely present to people. To mention just a few instances, he notices Zacchaeus hidden up in a tree and invites him to have dinner with him. He hears the call of the blind beggar by the roadside and responds with healing. He hears the cry of the penitent thief on the cross and says, "Today, you will be with me in paradise."

How often people come to us, children to parents, wives to husbands, friends to friends, trying to unload their burdens, and as we sit there listening, our minds and hearts are thousands of miles away. If we were completely present to each other, we would rightfully expect miracles to happen. To be completely present is to care; it is to love; it is to gain a most precious gift: understanding.

Dr. Paul Tournier in his book *A Doctor's Casebook* says that sometimes a patient says to him, "I admire the patience with which you listen to everything I tell you." Then he says, "It is not patience at all, it is interest."

True meeting and true dialogue take place only in the present moment when two persons are fully present to each other-especially parents and children.

Next time you are with your husband, wife, children or friend try to be completely present and watch a miracle happen.

Father Knows Best

On his day off a father volunteered to stay home to allow the wife to visit friends. In the course of her absence, he cared for the three children but was careful to note on a piece of paper everything he did for the children. The summary of his day ran as follows:

Answered questions starting with "Why?": 25 times.
Pulled sticky lollipop out of Junior's hair: 3 times.
Dried tears: 9 times.
Changed baby's diapers: 15 times.
Blew assorted noses: 11 times.
Answered door: 4 times-baker, grocer, milkman and paper boy. All said they would rather come back when you were home.
Attempts made at getting spoon of food into baby's mouth: 18 times. *Succeeded*: twice.
Tied shoelaces: 13 times.
Requested in kind voice that children be quiet: once.
Told children to stop shouting: 18 times.
Warned children not to cross street: 16 times.
Watched children cross the street: 32 times.
Children asked me 10 times: "When is mommy coming home?" I asked myself the same question every 4 minutes.
Number of times daddy will stay home with children again: *None*!

Absentee Fathers

We slave and sweat to buy and maintain a few feet of real

estate, or run a profitable business, or get ahead in this world somehow. We rush around in the mad pursuit of earthly pleasure, we dash from one place to the next, always on the go. But the finest treasure in our possession means little or nothing to us-our children. Oh yes, we provide for them-we give them food and clothing and shelter-and music lessons and expensive toys and weekly allowances. But we don't give them the most important thing: *ourselves*! A survey was made recently among three hundred 7th and 8th grade boys to discover how much time fathers and sons spent together. Each boy kept an accurate record of the time spent with his father. The boys who saw dad only at the dinner table comprised the largest group. A number of boys never saw their fathers for days at a time, some not even for weeks. The average time that father and son had alone together for an entire week was 7 ½ minutes! No wonder T.S. Eliot wrote: "We are rearing children whom we don't know, and who will never know us."

One of the great problems of the American family today is *absentee fathers*. Every child needs an adult of his own sex to guide him and serve as his model in growing up. This is what fathers are for. Yet it seems that fathers are so busy directing businesses and corporations that they're unable to manage their own households. They have lost the executive touch where it counts the most-right at home. How often we find men like Eli in the Old Testament. He was an excellent priest but a poor father. He had time for everything except his own boys.

When a judge was confronted with a 15-year-old kid in trouble, he made an unusual but very proper judgment. He sentenced the father to 30 days of dinner at home.

One evening a father returned home worried because his

business had failed. His little girl climbed on his knee and, embracing her dad, said, "Don't get rich again, Daddy. You did not come into the nursery when you were rich, but now we can come around you, and get on your knee and kiss you."

Approachable

The importance of spending time with one's children is that it makes father *approachable*. If father is approachable, children will want to come to him with their problems. A daughter learns her first attitudes about men from her father; and even how a son gets along in a men's world is affected by how well he got along with his father. Adults who cannot get along well with people can trace their problem back to a poor relationship with their parents. By learning to relate well to his parents, the child learns to relate well to others. But how can children learn all these things from father if he is unapproachable, if he is too busy to spend time with them?

Even mothers at times tend to separate father from the children. For example, a father comes home tired and worn out from the day's work. His wife tries to hold the children back whenever they try to make contact with him: "Daddy is very tired; we must leave him in peace." This is how mothers contribute to the breaking down of father's lines of communication with the children so that he slowly becomes the unapproachable one.

A young boy made this entry in his diary: "Went fishing with my father-the most glorious day of my life." And so great was the influence of this one day's personal experience with his father that for 30 years thereafter he made repeated references in his diary to the glowing memory of that day. But the boy's father made a different comment in his diary about the same day and incident: "Went fishing with my son. A day wasted!"

Praise

The second bit of advice to fathers is given by St. Paul when he writes: "Fathers, provoke not your children to wrath; but bring them up in the nurture and admonition of the Lord" (Eph. 6:4). Sometimes father is so stern and strict that the children are uneasy as long as he is around. When he leaves home they breathe a sigh of relief. What kind of image do we have as fathers? Do our children feel a joy when we're at home? Do they miss us when we're gone or do they feel relieved?

One father who had been constantly criticizing his son for his faults stood by his bed one night in deep remorse and wrote the following memorable confession:

"Listen, Son: I am saying this as you lie asleep, one little paw crumpled under your cheek . . .

"These are the things I was thinking, Son: I had been cross to you. I scolded you as you were dressing for school because you gave your face merely a dab with the towel . . . I called out angrily when you threw your things on the floor . . .

"At breakfast I found fault, too. You spilled things. You gulped your food. You put your elbows on the table. You spread the butter too thick on your bread. And as you started off to play, and I to work, you turned and waved a hand and called, 'Goodbye, Daddy,' and I frowned, and said in reply, 'Hold your shoulders back!'

"Then it began all over again in the later afternoon. As I came up the road I spied you, down on your knees, playing

marbles. There were holes in your stockings. I humiliated you before your friends by marching you ahead of me to the house. Stockings were expensive-and if you had to buy them you would be more careful! Imagine that, Son, from a father!
. . .

"Well, Son, it was shortly afterward that my paper slipped from my hands and a terrible sickening fear came over me. What has habit been doing to me? The habit of finding fault, of reprimanding-was this my reward to you for being a boy? It was not that I did not love you; it was that I expected too much. I was measuring you by the yardstick of my own years."

The writer concludes his confession with these words: "But tomorrow I will be a real daddy. I will spend time with you, and suffer when you suffer, and laugh when you laugh. I will bite my tongue when impatient words come. I will keep saying as if it were a ritual, 'He is nothing but a boy-a little boy-I have asked too much, too much.'"

How important it is to remember that God is not finished with any of us yet. He is still making us.

Respect

Some years ago a New York judge decided to visit the country which had the lowest delinquency rate in the world to see if he could find the reason for this. This is what he found:

"*The young people in this country respect authority* . . . I found that even in the house of the poorest laborer, the father was respected by the wife and the children as the head of the family. He was the leader of that family, and ruled his brood with varying degrees of love and tenderness and firmness.

His household had rules to live by, and the child who disobeyed them was punished." Thus this judge stated that one of the major cures for delinquency was: "*Put a father back at the head of the family.*"

The Bible teaches the same thing. In fact, that's where the whole idea comes from. In Ephesians 5:22 we read: "*Wives submit yourselves unto your own husbands, as unto the Lord. For the husband is the head of the wife, even as Christ is the head of the church.*" This is the way God has ordained for a well-ordered home. It means that father has an authority which has been given to him by God Himself. He is to represent God in the family. This is not man's idea but God's. God has appointed him as the head of the house, and He expects him to carry out his assignment in a manner that will honestly reflect the fatherhood of God, in spite of all natural human limitations.

Of course this presupposes that fathers are worthy of such respect. Unfortunately many of them are not. It is their fault that they have lost control over their households. The breakdown of authority in modern homes is due first of all not to the failure of children to respect their fathers but rather to the failure of the fathers to command that respect.

There used to be a very popular television program called "Father Knows Best." And on this program father always knew best, for things can usually be arranged that way on television. Everything turns out right in the end, so that father looks pretty good. But when does father know best?

He knows best when he spends time with his children, talks with them, encourages them, makes himself approachable so that they will feel free to come to him with their problems. Father knows best when he is not overly strict with his children, when he understands their mistakes but does not condone them, when he disciplines them but then loves them all the more. Father knows best when he places Christ first in his home-and doesn't let the children do all the praying at the supper table but takes time himself to lead his family in prayer as head of the home. Father knows best when he accepts humbly the place of honor God has assigned him in the family, when he represents God to his children, gives them a true picture of God, one that will make them love and obey God as their heavenly Father.

What One Father Did

A busy executive who frequently works evenings, often regretted that he wasn't able to do more things with his two young sons. For Christmas last year, he decided to give his children a gift of time.

He gave each boy a book of coupons redeemable on any Sunday afternoon. One coupon read, "Good for one game of Monopoly." Another said, "Good for a long hike in the woods." Still others were, "Good for making something together in my workshop," "Good for a game of badminton," and, "Good for reading you a story."

The boys were delighted. Each week they carefully deliberated over which coupon to turn in that Sunday. He found that, although he might have said NO if the boys had merely interrupted his reading with a vague request to "play with us," he thoroughly enjoyed redeeming the coupons.

The real reward came two months later on Valentine's Day. Both boys bubbled with excitement as they presented their valentines to their dad: two coupon books, lovingly decorated with red and pink crayon hearts and containing coupons good for, "Shine your shoes," "Wash the car" and "Bring you the Sunday paper in bed."

"Not If He's Like You, Dad"

A pastor once had a son who became seriously ill. After the boy had undergone an exhaustive series of tests, the father was told the shocking news that his son had a terminal illness. The father prayed with his boy. Then he gently told him that the doctors could promise him only a few more days to live. "Are you afraid to meet Jesus, my boy?" asked his devout father. Blinking away a few tears, the little fellow said bravely, "No, not if He's like you, Dad!"